UTSA PT LIBRARY

D0786975

WITHDRAWN
UTSA LIBRARIES

COPY

in **DETAIL** Semi-Detached and Terraced Houses

in **DETAIL**

Semi-Detached and Terraced Houses

Christian Schittich (Ed.)

with essays contributed by
Andrea Wiegelmann
Walter Stamm-Teske and Lars-Christian Uhlig
Patrick Jung

Edition DETAIL – Institut für internationale
Architektur-Dokumentation GmbH & Co. KG
München

Birkhäuser – Publishers for Architecture
Basel · Boston · Berlin

Editor: Christian Schittich
Co-Editor: Andrea Wiegelmann
Editorial services: Alexander Felix, Kathrin Draeger, Astrid Donnert,
Julia Liese, Michaela Linder, Christa Schicker, Melanie Schmid, Cosima Strobl

Translation German/English:
Catherine Anderle-Neill (pp. 38–176), Adam Blauhut (pp. 14–27)
Allison Brown (pp. 28–37), David Skogley (pp. 8–13)
ndrea Saiko
Drawings: Kathrin Draeger, Norbert Graeser, Marion Griese, Silvia Hollmann,
Claudia Hupfloher, Nicola Kollmann, Elisabeth Krammer,
Sabine Nowak, Andrea Saiko

DTP: Peter Gensmantel, Andrea Linke, Roswitha Siegler, Simone Soesters

A specialist publication from Redaktion DETAIL
This book is a cooperation between
DETAIL – Review of Architecture and
Birkhäuser – Publishers for Architecture

A CIP catalogue record for this book is available
from the Library of Congress, Washington D.C., USA

Bibliographic information published by Die Deutsche Bibliothek
The Deutsche Bibliothek lists this publication in the Deutsche
Nationalbibliografie; detailed bibliographic data is available on the Internet at
<http://dnb.ddb.de>.

This book is also available in a German language edition (ISBN 3-7643-7488-8).

© 2006 Institut für internationale Architektur-Dokumentation GmbH & Co. KG,
P.O. Box 33 06 60, D-80066 München, Germany and
Birkhäuser – Publishers for Architecture, P.O. Box 133, CH-4010 Basel,
Switzerland

This work is subject to copyright. All rights are reserved, whether the whole or
part of the material is concerned, specifically the rights of translation, reprinting,
re-use of illustrations, recitation, broadcasting, reproduction on microfilms or in
other ways, and storage in data banks. For any kind of use, permission of the
copyright owner must be obtained.

Printed on acid-free paper produced from chlorine-free pulp (TCF ∞)

Printed in Germany
Reproduction:
Martin Härtl OHG, München
Printing and binding:
Kösel GmbH & Co. KG, Altusried-Krugzell

ISBN 10: 3-7643-7489-6
ISBN 13: 978-3-7643-7489-1

9 8 7 6 5 4 3 2 1

Library
University of Texas
at San Antonio

Contents

Living in Terraced Housing

Andrea Wiegelmann

The wish to become a homeowner continues to be the most important objective in life for most people. Terraced housing and semidetached houses are a cost-effective and more ecological alternative to detached single-family houses, more affordable even for young families. In addition, urban living has once again become popular. Young people, singles, and professional couples without children are not the only ones who are more often remaining in the city. Families who prefer less commuting and better chances for child care to an automobile-dependent life on the periphery are also doing so. Rows of terraced housing, for example within existing housing blocks, offer these people the possibility of combining the wish to live within one's own four walls with the advantages of inner-city living. This is an option recognized also by an increasing number of elderly people, whose children have left home and who require an intact environment with an extensive net of services. Within this context inner-city vacant lots are gaining significance. They need to be developed, even if the critical budgetary situation of communities is often at odds with the short-term profit orientation of investors, which is not usually conducive to sustainable urban growth.

Having a home is a basic need and at the same time an expression of a cultural and social way of life. With our own place to live and choice of surroundings we create an environment to fit our needs. In a time when traditional family structures are dissolving in favor of more individual lifestyles, well-known forms of dwelling have lost their validity. Floor plans and housing typology now need to offer a platform for living to people who are constantly undergoing change and are involved in a great variety of living situations. The possibility for continuous change is in great demand. Changes in floor plan solutions mirror these new conditions, as pointed out in the article by Walter Stamm-Teske and Lars Christian Uhlig (see page 14ff.). The examples contained in this book also verify this.

But what actually is terraced and semidetached housing? How do the two differ from one another? How are they different from detached single-family houses or from houses in a row? Both terms describe single-family houses arranged in horizontal rows, whereas a row of semidetached houses is limited to two units. As opposed to detached single-family houses built in a row, which are distinguished by the varied design of their individual facades, each house in terraced and semidetached housing is integrated into a single ensemble through a uniform structuring of the facades. A common facade design is also possible, which means the individual house is then no longer recognizable as such. The compact method of construction limits the use of open space and reduces the size of the facade. Expenditures are thus reduced, enabling builders with smaller budgets to achieve their dream of home ownership. It also makes it easier to resell the house at a later date, an argument which is gaining in importance due to increasing mobility and more frequent changing of jobs. Your own house accompanies you through individual periods of your life. In Holland this is referred to as a "residential career".

In addition to a lower purchase price, owners can also save when building semidetached or terraced housing through efficient planning and construction and the use of prefabricated products. Here as well it is worth having a look at the Netherlands, where, after decades of total standardization, a gradual change is occurring. Many recently built terraced housing developments no longer offer buyers a completely finished product, but instead define a more or less neutral framework within which residents can develop as they wish. In addition to spending less money on the property and the building itself, with the proper planning of semidetached and terraced housing owners can also save on investments for utilities such as heating and solar systems. Having less exterior surfaces than a detached single-family house also leads to lower operational heating costs. Any proceeds from solar gain can be divided among neighbors (see p. 28ff., article by Patrick Jung).

All in all, terraced and semidetached housing represents a cost-effective and environmentally sound alternative to detached single-family houses. New and especially sustainable concepts are urgently needed if increased suburban sprawl is to be contained and new urban construction on vacant land promoted, while satisfying the changing living situations.

1.2

1.3

1.4

The History of the Terraced House

Terraced housing is one of the oldest residential building forms and can be traced back to antiquity. While this category of building can look back at a tradition more than 3000 years old, the semidetached house is a relatively new residential building type, which first emerged during the nineteenth century in England as a result of the garden city movement.

Throughout its history the terraced house was adapted time and time again to changing social and economic conditions; it was an experimental area for architects and planners and was thus instrumental to the further development of the typology of housing. The following examples illustrate the essential developmental phases.

The ancient Egyptians surrounded their strongly typified terraced houses with walls and used them as accommodation for workers. Early examples are found in Greece as well, such as the *insulae* with stansardized housing in Piraeus built in 480 BCE by the Greek architect, urban planner, and philosopher Hippodames of Milet.

While the aforementioned examples concern dense groups of terraced housing, whole neighborhoods, or in the case of workers' housing in Egypt, entire towns the terraced houses we are familiar with – a sequence of single residential buildings in a row built by a single client according to a standardized plan – developed from the so-called *Gottesbuden* (small rent-free buildings for the poor), which were socially motivated developments of uniform rows divided into single houses. Foundations, wealthy citizens, and usually, employers, provided housing for poor citizens, workers, and impoverished craftsmen, which served not least as a way of maintaining the workforce. One of the best known examples is the Fuggerei in Augsburg, built in 1519. The systematically laid out development just outside the gates of the city included the prototype of a small apartment oriented toward the basic necessities, and was socially and architecturally exemplary for its time (fig. 1.2, 1.3).

Comparable developments of small, uniformly constructed houses organized in rows were also built in Cologne, Nuremberg and later in Strasbourg, Mainz, Amsterdam (the so-called béguinage), Ghent, Utrecht, Leiden, and Haarlem. As the economy improved and trade relations expanded, cities and settlements also continued to develop. As commerce and trade grew in importance, medieval cities soon became too small for the rapid growth of their populations. In order to put off the construction of new defensive walls for as long as possible, construction within the existing walls became increasingly dense; tall, narrow town houses, built according to uniform standards for a great variety of groups within the population, marked the streets and squares with their characteristic facades. Detached houses were visually joined together according to specific design guidelines. This urban variation of terraced housing is found in all important commercial centers. In the course of urban expansion between the second and third rings in Bologna's city wall at the beginning of the eleventh century, large blocks of housing were built which consisted of narrow, 3.8- to 6-meter-wide terraced housing for craftsmen and workers.

In Wurzburg a street with two and three-story terraced houses, each having two apartments, was built between 1747 and 1750 for court officials according to plans by Balthasar Neumann. The houses were visually linked through a unified facade design, forming a single visual unit. Parallel to this, the model of urban detached houses built in a row was developed. Design guidelines were used here as well to create a framework within which the facades were designed individually, so that each house was clearly visible. An example of this is Amsterdam's urban expansion in the early seventeenth century. The area between the three large, newly laid out canals was divided into narrow plots; the buildings' remarkable facades continue to characterize the townscape to today. After the revolution in 1689, England developed into the most powerful trading nation in Europe; London surpassed Amsterdam as the commercial and financial center. The English metropolis was the first city in which construction was no longer financed by the government or a small upper class but by a large number of private initiatives. The first English terraced houses were built in the eighteenth century for the aristocracy and the upper classes: a row of houses formed the terrace, a group of detached houses with individual floor plans and similar facades, which appeared as a single entity on the street. Well-known examples of this type are found in English bathing resorts, like the semicircular residential development with thirty terraced houses built between 1867 and 1875 around a plaza in Bath by John Wood, Jr. The middle and the ends are discreetly accentuated, so that the ensemble in its entirety resembles an oval palace facade. The rapid economic changes that came with the industrial revolution led to new societal structures by the end of the eighteenth century. From then on the urban population was divided into industrialists and workers. Living conditions for industrial workers drastically worsened as a result of the enormous need for labor and the large migration to the cities. In reaction to this deplorable state of affairs, industrial housing developments were created – once again initiated by employers – which later led to garden cities. Whereas the industrial housing developments created by industrialists were often extremely purposeful and uniform for reasons of profitability, garden cities were supposed to combine the advantages of urban living with those of country life. Beginning with Ebenezer Howard and his *Garden Cities of Tomorrow* (1898), the movement expanded within Europe and America. The first garden city in Germany was built in Hellerau between 1906 and 1914. Through the initiative of the Dresden furniture manufacturer Karl Schmidt, Richard Riemerschmid and Heinrich Tessenow were able to create an extremely varied catalog of single-family terraced and semi-detached housing. In 1908, during the planning phase, Tessenow developed a concept for small apartments in which the houses had a width of only 4.5 meters.

While garden cities were consciously sited outside cities, in the 1920s an innovative planning model was developed for urban living, which proclaimed a new lifestyle and social-hygienic standards: facing the sun, the apartments were well lit and had sufficient cross-ventilation. Ernst May, as the head of municipal planning and building in Frankfurt (1926–1930), was especially resolute in implementing this. Under his management the "New Frankfurt" was developed, the large-scale

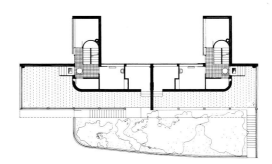

1.5

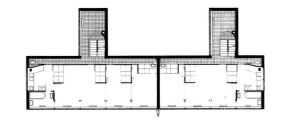

1.6

1.7

1.1   Urban terraced housing in London
1.2   View of terraced houses, Fuggerei Augsburg, 1519
1.3   Floor plan, ground floor, Fuggerei Augsburg, 1519
1.4   Terraced houses, Weißenhofsiedlung Stuttgart, 1927, J. J. P. Oud
1.5   Floor plan, ground floor, semi-detached houses, Weißenhofsiedlung Stuttgart, 1927, Le Corbusier,
1.6   Floor plan, first floor, semi-detached houses, Weißenhofsiedlung Stuttgart, 1927, Le Corbusier,
1.7   Doppelhaus, Weißenhofsiedlung Stuttgart, 1927, Le Corbusier

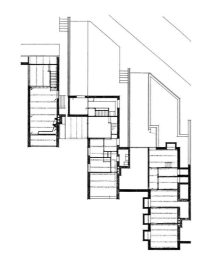

1.8

1.9

planning of residential developments for the lower classes. In this context the Praunheim subsidized public housing development (Reichsheimstättensiedlung) was built, which consisted of terraced housing with rooftop and house gardens. The two- and three-story units have standardized floor plans; the building process was greatly rationalized through the use of large construction panels. May arranged all rooms hierarchically, thus reorganizing the floor plans. Living rooms and kitchens became essential common rooms within the houses. One of the most important projects in this context is Stuttgart's Weissenhofsiedlung, which was built in 1927 as the building exhibition for the Deutscher Werkbund (German Work Federation) with the goal of presenting exemplary new forms of living for modern people. Groundbreaking projects built according to Ludwig Mies van der Rohe's urban master plan, experimented with new types of construction materials and methods. Architects Le Corbusier and Pierre Jeanneret were responsible for one of the housing development's most well-known projects, the Doppelhaus (a pair of semidetached houses), built in 1927. Both semidetached houses are designed with an optimized floor plan of minimal size, which can be adapted to a variety of uses through flexible fixtures and fittings. The floor plans resemble the space-saving arrangement of railroad cars (fig. 1.5–1.7). J. J. P. Oud also worked on the functional organization of the floor plans. He used experience gained from working on the Kiefhoek development in Rotterdam, which was being planned at the same time, and built affordable apartments adapted to the needs of the masses. The floor plans have hardly any connecting hallways; living and working areas are clearly separated and functionally connected to one another. Kitchens, pantries and other functional areas face north to the street;, the large living area faces south to the yard (fig. 1.4).

In Vienna Adolf Loos dealt with the problem of terraced houses' limited options for expansion. Between 1921 and 1924 a model development was built on the Heuberg hill according to his concept of the "growing house". His concept for increasing the size of the house mainly involved rebuilding and extending the upper story.

Further development in housing construction was dealt a major blow by the Second World War. Even though the benefits of serial production were taken advantage of after 1945, and countless small housing developments were built parallel to the reconstruction of cities, due to the acute shortage of housing these were usually monotonous, serially produced neighborhoods. There are examples, however, which attempted to satisfy the increasing demands of residents, thus giving the development of terraced housing a fresh impetus.

In the 1950s and 1960s this momentum came from Scandinavia. Arne Jacobsen's Søholm residential development in Klampenborg, built between 1950 and 1955, is a lively ensemble created by staggering the buildings and inclined roofs, which provides residents with protected open areas despite the development's high building density (fig. 1.8). With the Kingo developments in Helsingør (1956–60) and Fredensborg (1962–63), Jørn Utzon also proved to be one of the housing sector's groundbreaking architects.

In Switzerland the architects of the Atelier 5 group have set new standards through their residential developments. The problem of creating a protected private zone in spite of proximity to neighbors was solved in an exemplary way at the Halen (1955–61) and Thalmatt 1 (1967–74) developments. The narrow buildings, which have individual floor plans, each have private outdoor areas through the ingenious arrangement of the buildings and skillful exploitation of the hillside site.

In the 1980s, as a result of the oil crisis and a growing environmental consciousness, many projects focused on energy efficient and ecological construction in addition to social aspects. Metron Architects dealt with the possibility of passive solar use with their housing development in Röthenbach on the Pegnitz, built as part of Wohnmodelle Bayern (Model Housing in Bavaria) project in 1990. The Quartier Steinberg, a model development with 54 units, was built with an eye to an optimum southern orientation. The buildings are almost 6.4 meters long; additional rooms were created as a buffer zone facing north. In order to maximize the solar heat gain the gently pitched pent roofs are sloped to the north.

The development built in 1989 by Hermann Schröder and Sampo Widman in Passau-Neustift as part of the same model project consists of terraced houses that are 3.9 meters wide and 13.9 meters long. In order to use passive solar energy in spite of the long and narrow floor plans, simple glass-enclosed porches were built on the southern side to trap and store the sun's energy. Different-sized apartments were created in buildings of the same width by varying the number of stories and changing the layout of rooms.

New variations of urban terraced housing have arisen parallel to these model developments. Numerous projects were built in the Netherlands. The renaissance of this type of house was motivated to a certain degree by West 8's urban master plan for Borneo Sporenburg. Based on Amsterdam's old urban quarters a new urban neighborhood was created which is characterized by homogeneous rows of housing and structured by individual monumental buildings. The quarter's foundation is the patio house, which found a variety of interpretations by the different architects involved in the project. In 1998 Kees Christiaanse built an ensemble consisting of 44 three-story town houses. Due to the narrow floor plan and small site (the width of each house is 4.2 meters), he was able to achieve an architectural density comparable to multi-story housing. The design of the floor plan meets the aim of mixed use, with offices on the ground floor and apartments on the upper floors. A secluded rooftop terrace provides private outdoor space (fig. 1.9).

Projects such as the Quartier McNair in the Steglitz district of Berlin demonstrate an additional possibility for building on vacant urban land. The site of a former army barracks has been developed according to a strict system of semidetached and terraced housing. Carlo Baumschlager and Dietmar Eberle, together with Anatole du Fresne, a former member of Atelier 5, developed the urban planning concept, which allows for a great degree of variation within a rigidly set framework. The two- and three-story terraced houses are joined together in rows of five to eight units of varying widths. Various floor plans can be combined according to the wishes of residents (Fig. 1.10).

Terraced housing and semidetached housing have been interpreted anew at both Borneo Sporenburg and the Quartier McNair. Both examples demonstrate solutions which do justice to existing residential needs. It is no coincidence that they are found in an urban context. The importance of the urban residential form is growing in view of increasing demand. The future of residential development lies in urban and suburban areas, the context within which both types of housing were ultimately created.

1.10

Bibliography

Atelier 5. *Siedlungen und städtebauliche Projekte.* Braunschweig/Wiesbaden 1994

Benevolo, Leonardo. *Die Geschichte der Stadt.* 8th ed.. Frankfurt/New York 2000

Faller, Peter. *Der Wohnungsgrundriss.* Stuttgart/München 2002

Flagge, Ingeborg, ed. *Geschichte des Wohnens Band 5. 1945- heute Aufbau, Neubau, Umbau.* Stuttgart: 1999

Harlander, Tilman, ed. *Villa und Eigenheim – Suburbaner Städtebau in Deutschland.* Ludwigsburg: Stuttgart/München 2001

Lampugnani, Vittorio Magnago, ed. *Lexikon der Architektur des 20. Jahrhunderts.* Ostfildern-Ruit 1998

Oberste Bayerische Baubehörde, ed. *Wohnmodelle Bayern 1984–1990.* München: 1990

Stamm-Teske, Walter, ed. *Preiswerter Wohnungsbau in den Niederlanden 1993–1998.* Düsseldorf: 1998

Thau, Carsten, Vindum, Kjeld. *Arne Jacobsen.* Copenhagen 2002

Uhlig, Lars-Christian, Stamm-Teske, Walter, eds. *Neues Bauen am Horn. Eine Mustersiedlung in Weimar.* Leipzig 2005

Van Gool, Rob, Hertelt, Lars, Raith, Frank-Bertolt, Schenk, Leonhard. *Das niederländische Reihenhaus. Serie und Vielfalt.* Stuttgart 2000

Wüstenrot Stiftung, ed. *Das städtische Reihenhaus.Geschichte und Typologie.* Stuttgart/Zürich 2004

Wüstenrot Stiftung, ed. *Wohnbauen in Deutschland.* Stuttgart/Zürich 2000

1.8   Floor plan, basement, ground floor and first floor, terraced housing, Søholm I, Denmark, 1950, Arne Jacobsen
1.9   Townhouses, Sporenburg, Amsterdam, 1998, Kees Christianse
1.10   Quartier McNair residential developement, Berlin, 2002, d-company architects in cooperation with Baumschlager & Eberle

From Villa to Terraced House Typological Observations on Semi-detached and Terraced Homes

By Walter Stamm-Teske und Lars-Christian Uhlig

When exploring the possibility of owning their own home, many people are forced to realize that they lack the financial means for their ideal dwelling – a detached single-family house. In other cases, urban planning constraints make it impossible to build this type of house at the desired location. Semidetached and terraced houses are a viable alternative. They generally cost less, and they can be adapted to a variety of planning contexts, from suburban villa neighborhoods to high-density street-side urban developments.

Many people believe a detached single-family house is the only way to satisfy their need for privacy and sufficient space between themselves and their neighbors, and to express their individuality. It is indeed a paradox that mass-produced houses bought "off the shelf" and constructed in identical versions across the country are favored over individually designed semidetached and terraced homes that represent adequate urban planning solutions but are regarded as lacking individuality and reining in creative freedoms.

One of the largest German real estate services on the Web offers potential homeowners definitions of basic terminology revolving around home construction. The definitions of the terms "semidetached house" and "terraced house" reveal how they are perceived by buyers and sellers.

"The semidetached house is a compromise between a detached single-family house and a terraced dwelling. Semidetached houses can be built on narrow plots. … In contrast to terraced and linked housing, they have an open space on the sides and closely resemble single-family dwellings. Both units have an identical layout and are connected along a party wall. …

"The problems associated with semidetached houses include relations with neighbors, a certain compulsion to adapt designs to that of the building next door, and the separation of the outdoor space from the neighbor. Architects must deal with these problem sensitively in the planning stage."[1]

This passage clearly shows that many people regard semidetached houses as a compromise. They have open spaces on one side and an outdoor area that is just 20 percent smaller than that of a detached house, but the cheaper costs for heating, shared utilities and waste removal hardly make up for the disadvantages, which include disturbance by the neighbors and the obligatory design adaptations. In a worst-case scenario, semidetached homes are sold only after they have been completed, to buyers who might not even know each other. In an ideal scenario – which goes unmentioned in the above passage – semidetached houses can be jointly designed and constructed by two parties who desire proximity and intend to share outdoor areas that are more spacious than those surrounding single-family homes.

"Terraced housing consists of rows of narrow, deep homes two to three stories tall. Each building in the terrace represents an individual housing unit. The interiors often feature a split-level design that is well suited to deep structures.

"Terraced houses utilize the entire land area extremely efficiently. They can be built on very small plots, which saves money. …"[2]

The terraced house is portrayed more positively than semidetached houses since it is assumed that builders or buyers have a small budget and are forced to economize. The definition mentions architectural solutions such as split levels or projections and recessions that can improve natural lighting conditions and facilitate a freer design of the structure. However, there is no mention of the possible advantages of wide house types (see "House width and depth").

This essay describes how semidetached and terraced homes can be adapted to a variety of basic conditions and occupant requirements without having to revert to standardized products. Both the proximity of the units and the need to preserve individual spaces present architects with a special challenge. Even so, the potential for material and energy savings as well as for efficient use of space remains undisputed.

Typologies

Semidetached and terraced houses are house types which, in terms of their floor-plan design, closely resemble the detached single-family house as the smallest unit of residential housing. In other words, they are normally several stories tall, integrated vertically from top to bottom, and autonomous on their portion of a lot. This distinguishes them from Germany's historical "villas" – an upper-middle-class house with a yard that in the past was divided into several housing units

2.1   Sound barrier terraced housing in Hilversum, 2001; Maurice NIO

15

2.2

(for the family, servants, etc.) and organized as one large household. And it also sets them apart from residential buildings in which the apartments are stacked above one another or extend across several levels but are not vertically integrated.

The type of twin house that is most common today – a free-standing dwelling divided into two separate units with mirror-image floor plans – evolved in the nineteenth century. The villas built in neighborhoods outside the perimeters of German cities included not only freestanding structures, but also attached houses that were known as "double houses" (Doppelhäuser).[3] While it is true that each of these units had only three outside walls instead of the usual four, their advantage was that they required a much smaller piece of property and were less expensive to build than detached homes with yards (the traditional villa). Residents still had direct access to their backyards by walking around the house, and the interior received natural light along three sides.

Terraced housing first emerged when additional units were connected along their side walls. Here the house on the end of the row has the character of a semidetached dwelling. The terraced houses in the middle normally have a smaller piece of property and windows at the front and back, and the yard behind the house is separated from the front yard and street. This house type existed in the nineteenth century, with larger versions known as "row villas" (Reihenvilla).

The concept of a public garden city spread in the period before the First World War, paving the way for a shift from neighborhoods of upper-middle-class villas to simple housing developments consisting of smaller homes.[4] Architects were able to lower constructions costs by streamlining and standardizing floor plans, and, above all, by building terraced housing and groups of dwellings.

As a result of both industrialization and the housing shortage following the First World War, there was a growing demand for inexpensive new housing that could satisfy the need for fresh air and sunlight. The terraced house – which could be produced "like cars on an assembly line"[5] – lent itself well to meeting these needs. The exponents of the Neues Bauen movement developed "model homes" that could be built with standardized components and production methods. At the same time, the basic patterns of urban development changed: terraced houses were arranged in long rows to facilitate construction of identical units. The houses on the end, known as end terraces, had no special design since planners were concerned with producing one house type, the middle unit. This trend in planning was not without negative consequences: the loss of articulated street space and city squares.

In addition to developing standardized terraced homes, the architects of Neues Bauen created sophisticated designs for terraced houses and optimized semidetached housing. One example is the twin house designed by Le Corbusier in the Weißenhof estate in Stuttgart. A particularly interesting development can be seen in the master houses of Walter Gropius in Dessau (fig. 2.2, 2.3). The three twin houses by Klee and Kandisky, Muche and Schlemmer, and Feininger and Moholy-Nagy feature mirror-image floor plans twisted 90

2.3

degrees. The resulting shape takes the twin house back to its original form as a villa: a large house conceived as a whole yet divided into two individual units. Over the last few years there have been several new examples of semidetached homes in which the overall design is much more important than the distinguishability of the individual units and property boundaries. The point of departure is often a neighborhood of appropriately sized villas. Inside, the homes form differently zoned units (fig. 2.6). In other houses, room orientation changes by the floor (fig. 2.4, 2.5). There are also examples of houses that incorporate different-sized units that are either inhabitable separately with an in-law apartment, or are partially or fully integrated as multigenerational homes.

There is also a trend today toward introducing variety into the design of identical rows of terraced housing and making the individual homes more distinct. These new housing developments frequently quote historical forms such as the Brandevoort or Slot Haverleij in the Netherlands, which are based on the master plans of the Krier and Kohl architectural office.[6] One example of this type of modern design is the Bloemenweide[7] in Ypenburg near The Hague, a large site that is part of the Dutch government's VINEX program.[8] Based on a master plan by West 8, four acclaimed architectural firms[9] developed different terraced homes that are combined in a varied way. Together with the clear material and design specifications, this mix creates a consistent overall impression that is lacking in the otherwise monotonous rows of terraced houses on the other VINEX sites.

The focus on a single plot permits even greater variety and individuality, as shown by townhouses along historical city streets. In this case, the individual buildings are designed by different architects in compliance with architectural specifications (height, width, depth, materials, roof shape, etc.). Most of these "housing developments" take the form of terraced housing in urban contexts. Examples include the Scheepstimmermanstraat in Amsterdam[10] (fig. 2.8) and Trier-Petrisberg. The combination of enclosed and semi-open, divergent designs in Adolf Krischanitz's development plan for the Neues Bauen am Horn project in Weimar proves that a twin house can also take the form of two individually designed homes[11] that share one wall and allow for interspersed green areas, as in a garden city (fig. 2.9).

Home living

Other authors have provided exemplary, comprehensive descriptions of the different functional areas of modern floor plans,[12] so we will limit ourselves in what follows to the special aspects of multistory living in semidetached and terraced houses.

Entrance area
The entrance area marks the interface between exterior and interior, between public and private space. If semidetached

2.4

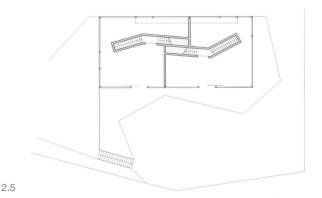

2.5

2.6

2.2 Muche/Schlemmer house in Dessau, 1927, Refurbishment 2002; Walter Gropius
2.3 Axonometry, Muche/Schlemmer house in Dessau, 1927, Walter Gropius
2.4 Twin house in Bischoffweg, Riehen, 2003; Morger & Degelo
2.5 First floor and ground floor plan, twin house in Bischoffweg, Riehen, 2003; Morger & Degelo
2.6 Twin house "Villa KBWW," Utrecht ,1977; MVRDV

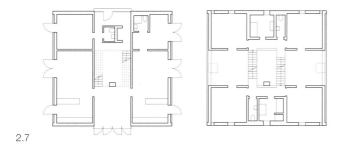

2.7

and terraced homes have the usual front yard, there is already a spatial separation between these two spheres and greater privacy for the house entrance. If this entrance is situated directly on the street in an urban context, or if the entrances of a pair of semidetached homes are very close together, special attention must be paid to protecting this private sphere from unwanted disturbances (see "Secondary structures"). In the city, this can be achieved by raising the ground floor above the sidewalk. It is easier to accept and enjoy a window overlooking the street if the eye level of a person sitting in the house is higher than that of passers by. Direct contact with the street environment is an important requirement for both urban design and social relations.

A crucial point when planning pathways and additional functional areas in a home is whether the entrance floor will contain the communal spaces (kitchen, dining area, living room, etc.). If not, the entrance can be designed as a place for a wardrobe or a closet. The guest toilet that is otherwise located there should then be placed closer to the communal areas, ideally on the same floor. The path that leads to the communal areas via the hall and stairway should be as direct as possible and not disturb the bedrooms.

If the communal areas are located on the entrance floor, it is essential that this floor also include a toilet, which can share the same building services as the kitchen. This will preserve the privacy of the bedrooms if the other floors are accessed directly via a stairway from the entrance area or hall. It will also make it possible to divide the house into two units (multi-generational living), as in the cooperative development in Weimar.

Kitchen/dining area
There is a close functional relationship between kitchen and dining areas, and these should be situated side by side on the same floor – not only because cooking has now become an important leisure-time activity, but also because communication between the kitchen and dining area is always important, either when cooking with friends or the family. An ideal setup is to link the dining area to an outdoor sitting area for use during the warm months of the year.

A variety of solutions are possible, from a pure working kitchen that is separated from the dining room (or the dining/living area), to the integration of all cooking functions into the living area. First-time residents can create various spatial relations between the kitchen and eating areas that do not require a different layout of the service shaft. An excellent example is the terraced housing in Darmstadt, which features differently arranged kitchen units (see p. 66ff.).

Living area/outdoor spaces
An important spatial relationship exists between the interior common areas and the private exterior space, where people are now spending more and more time in the summer months. This inside space can take the form of a traditional living room (whose importance is currently declining, even in family life[13]) or a multifunctional area for a wide range of activities, including eating, cooking, playing, and celebrating. The opening between this room and its uncovered outdoor counterpart should be as wide as possible. Whereas outside space used to be designed as a backyard with a sitting area,

2.8

it can now include a roof terrace with sensational views, an enclosed garden courtyard, or an intimate atrium.

A whole series of different outdoor spaces are possible. With their highly communicative character, on the ground level they establish a direct relationship with both neighboring areas (yard, joint entrance area) and public space. Balconies on the upper floor ensure even greater privacy, and utter seclusion can be enjoyed on a roof terrace, as is impressively shown by the terraced homes in Küsnacht with their carefully designed outdoor spaces. The denser the development, the greater the importance of this private area on the roof terrace.

If this intimacy is to be preserved, neighbors should see as little of one another as possible. In twin houses, this goal can be easily achieved by giving the spaces different orientations. In terraced homes, projecting and recessed sections of the facade can be used to create niches for terraces and to direct natural light into the interior of deep buildings (see the housing complex in Gouda by KCAP).

Bedrooms/bathrooms
Over the last few years, the functional demands placed on bedrooms have transformed them into personal areas where residents can retreat from the world. The term "children's room," in particular, should be viewed critically. First of all, the ten years of childhood is a relatively short period of time compared to the lifecycle of a building; second, when children become teenagers, they place demands on their rooms that are similar to those placed on shared apartments.

This is one reason bedrooms are increasingly becoming "apartments within an apartment"[14] in modern homes. They serve as multifunctional living spaces, sleeping areas and studies that must be large enough to meet the full range of requirements. Peter Faller[15] recommends allotting a minimum of 14 square meters of living space to these multipurpose rooms, which can be furnished with a double or single bed and designed as a living area and combination kitchen/ dining room. Hannes Weeber and Simone Bosch[16] suggest a minimum room size of 4.10 × 4.10 m for sustainable use. Two beds can be placed next to each other on one side of the room or the room can be partitioned.

An example of a project that incorporates this basic module is the semidetached housing in Müllheim designed by the Freiburg architectural office of Pfeifer Roser Kuhn (fig. 2.7). The rooms here are all the same size and arranged in a ring around a spacious staircase hallway. When designing the LBS-Systemhaus (see p. 136ff.), the architects at G.A.S.-Sahner assumed that different combinations of the room modules, each measuring 15 square meters, could be attached to the required basic modules containing an entrance area and a bathroom/toilet. Different house types can be built with this system: not only freestanding, linked, and grouped dwellings but also semidetached, terraced, or atrium homes. Subsequent extensions are also possible. In narrow, deep terraced houses, the bedrooms are normally

2.9

2.7 Ground floor and first floor plan, twin house in Müllheim, 2005; Pfeifer Roser Kuhn
2.8 Scheepstimmermanstraat, Borneo, Amsterdam
2.9 Houses by Arndt and Ihlenfeld, Weimar, 2002; AFF Architekten

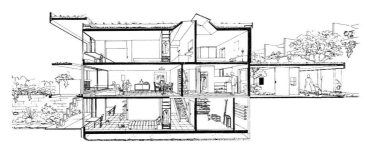

2.10

not square, but rectangular, extending into the depth of the house. The poorly lit areas in the interior can be used for walk-in closets so as to free up the better lit areas for other uses.

Bedrooms offer a great deal of privacy if they have direct access to a bathroom, as in the semidetached houses in Münchenstein or the terraced homes in Hilversum. An interesting, cost-effective solution can be seen in the terraced houses in Viken (see p. 50ff.), in which a shared shower room can be reached either through the family bathroom or via a separate washing area serving one bedroom directly.

The significance of the bathroom has increased dramatically over the past few decades. Once an essential area for personal hygiene, it has now evolved into a spacious wellness and fitness facility. Modern homes usually have a fully furnished bathroom on every bedroom floor. For a broad cross-section of the population, natural lighting is an important aspect of bathroom design,[17] though technically speaking, windows are no longer necessary thanks to mechanical ventilation systems with waste heat recovery. If a bathroom cannot be positioned along the outer wall in a building with a deep floor plan, a skylight should be used on upper floors to let in natural light.

Secondary structures and parking spaces
In addition to interior spaces, semidetached and terraced houses usually have private exterior spaces on their property that can be used for a variety of purposes. The adept integration of storage spaces for bikes, baby carriages, lawn and garden equipment, garbage containers, etc., can create a differentiated transition from the public street environment to the private house entrance. It can also make the front yard into a kind of buffer zone that is suitable for lingering and informal contacts (fig. 2.10).

For urban planning reasons (noise, poor view), the front yard can be enclosed to improve the quality of life. The individual terraced homes in the development in München-Harlaching stand on the edge of the site. They were shifted close to the street – from which they are separated by a wall – in order to preserve the park-like backyards. Intimate front courtyards have emerged that are linked to the kitchen and dining area. Communication is still possible through a gate in the wall near the house entrance (fig. 2.14).

It is often difficult to integrate parking spaces into the immediate living environment due to car emissions or for design reasons. The only place to park a car on the property surrounding a terraced home is the area directly in front of the house or in the structure itself. The parked car or a (prefabricated) garage impedes communication from the house to the street environment. Designs that enhance the quality of life include house entrances that can be reached by car for transport purposes, and parking spaces that are located at the edge of the row or even in a shared underground parking lot – as illustrated by the above-mentioned terraced housing development in München-Harlaching.

West 8 came up with an intriguing solution in Bloemenweide,[18] where the terraced houses stand on the edge of the street and are accessible via a rear alleyway. Parking spaces and garden sheds are also situated there (fig. 2.11).

2.11

If houses on sloping plots are accessed from the valley side, the required foundation can house a garage, as shown by the terraced homes in Küsnacht, where the planted garage roofs form a front yard and outdoor sitting area.

The semidetached houses in Münchenstein, designed by the architects Steinmann & Schmid, demonstrate that garages can be integrated into the house in a superb architectural design. This is important, since cars play a central role in the way homeowners present themselves. The high-quality materials (stainless steel), the architectural link to the main structure, as well as the planted pergola all around the garage roof terrace show that the architecture has higher aspirations than merely protecting cars from the elements.

Although the subject has been repeatedly discussed, there are no good examples of carports that have been integrated into the house in the form of an open multipurpose hall (e.g. garage/greenhouse).

House width and depth

Due to the distance to the neighbors next door, semidetached houses are normally found in suburban environments and surrounded by green. Since residents can access the yard and let in light on all sides, these buildings can have either a north-south or an east-west orientation, or they can feature asymmetrical designs oriented to all sides. By contrast, terraced houses are characterized by a rigid division between the front and backyards, and the two areas can have entirely different designs. Since terraced houses with an east-west orientation receive sunlight in the morning and evening, they normally have much deeper floor plans (10–14 meters) than houses with a north-south orientation (7–10 meters), which only receive sunlight from the south. If the urban context makes a deep north-south house necessary, an ideal solution is an atrium house that lets in light through a second southern facade.

2.12

The relationship between the orientation and width/depth of semidetached and terraced housing varies with different house types.

One room wide; double-flight or semi-circular stairway
The narrowest house type is a terraced home that is only one room wide. This means that there is only one room on each side of the house, and the stairway and bathrooms are situated in the center, where there is little direct daylight. Thus this house type is relatively deep. If it is two stories tall and the entrance area is connected to both the kitchen and the dining area, residents have three additional rooms that can be put to a variety of uses.

2.13

2.14

This house type is bested suited for west-east orientations since the morning and evening sun, hanging low in the sky, casts light deep into the rooms (fig. 2.12).

2.10 Sectional perspective, Halen, Herrenschwanden near Bern, 1961; Atelier 5
2.11 Terraced houses in Quarter 6, Bloemenweiden, Ypenburg, 2003; West 8 landscape artists
2.12 First floor plan, terraced houses in Göppingen, 1999; Wick & Partner
2.13 First floor plan, terraced housing development in Gouda, 2002; KCAP architects & planners
2.14 Terraced housing development in Munich, 2001; von Seidlein

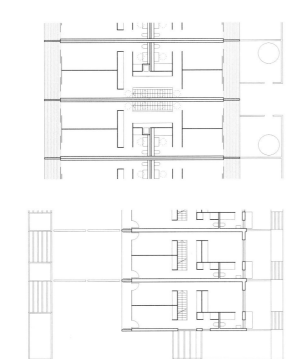

2.15

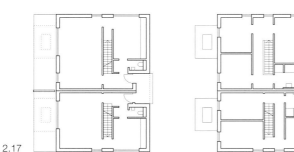

2.16

One room wide, stairway parallel to side wall
If the house is slightly wider, the entrance area can be placed next to the rooms. The stairway – usually a single-flight design – can receive light via openings in one or both facades, which gives the hallway the quality of a common area. In this case, the hallway can serve as a studio, playroom or library. If the stairway receives light from one side only, the rooms can have different sizes, which frequently results in a (large) bedroom for parents and a (small) children's room. However, it is advisable for the rooms to have a similar size to ensure flexible room assignments.

This house type is also well suited for east-west orientations, but it is normally not as deep as the house with a stairway at the core. Otherwise it would result in a overly large entrance area. In the residential complex in Gouda designed by KCAP, the entrance area next to the rooms is shorter, allowing for a small and a large terrace on the sides of the house (fig 2.13).

Two rooms wide, stairway parallel to side wall
Like the one-room-wide design, the two-room-wide house with a stairway in the center lends itself well to very deep floor plans with an east-west orientation. The housing development in München-Harlaching shows that, even in a house that is extremely deep, the central stairway can be lit and directly linked to outside space through skylights and by aligning room doors with the flight of stairs. The single-flight stairway is long enough to provide space for two bathrooms for the bedrooms on each side of the house. Since the interior walls are not load bearing, they can be removed to create one room on each side with direct access to the bathrooms. Ceilings must span the entire width of the house, so their dimensions place limits on room and house width (fig. 2.15).

Two rooms wide, perpendicular stairway
Due to its length and the landings on both sides, the single-flight, perpendicular stairway requires a very wide house. Two bedrooms can normally be arranged side by side and reached via the landings. In most cases, the bathroom runs from the stairway at the house core to the facade and is supplied with direct sunlight. One version of the terraced homes in Darmstadt features back-to-back bathrooms: whereas the small bath in the center receives no direct sunlight, the more spacious bathroom next to it, which is entered via one bedroom, has a window. In other variations, the same space is used for a single, large family bathroom (fig. 2.16).

The development in Ostfildern-Scharnhauser Park, designed by Fink+Jocher, is evidence that the same typology is found in semidetached houses. Here the hallway on the upper floor can receive light via openings in the third facade. In the three-story model, the hall next to the stairway switches position from the first to the second floor, making possible entirely different room sizes (for guest rooms, offices, etc.). An extremely efficient solution is the use of a single shaft for all building services. This house type lends itself well to both east-west and north-south orientations, as can be seen by layouts in urban contexts (see p.146; fig. 2.17).

Two rooms wide; double-flight or semi-circular stairway
A typical feature of terraced houses with a north-south orien-

2.17

tation is that they are wider than they are deep. The bedrooms and communal areas are situated on the southern side. Since the high southern sun does not shine deep into the room, bedrooms are usually square or rectangular with their longer side running along the facade. As shown by the terraced houses in Stuttgart designed by the architects Kohlmayer Oberst, the ground floor on the northern side can feature an entranceway connected to the double-flight or semi-circular stairway and a toilet and the kitchen. In this design, the bathroom on the upper floor is located directly above the kitchen (fig. 2.20).

Two rooms wide, stairway parallel to side wall
Terraced houses are wider and not as deep if a straight, single-flight stairway is located between the rooms. On the ground floor, this stairway normally separates the cooking/eating area from the living room – as in the terraced houses in the Röthenbach development.[19] The bathroom and a few secondary rooms are situated in the north. However, if the house is not very deep, the rooms on the upper floor may run from facade to facade since they can be reached directly from the stairway landing.

A disadvantage of this house type is that the bedrooms on the upper floor can only be accessed via the communal areas on the ground floor. Residents cannot reach them directly from a hallway leading from the house entrance (fig. 2.18)

Two rooms wide, double-flight or semi-circular stairway
A striking division into two halves can be found in houses with a double-flight or semi-circular staircase between two room axes. This increases the privacy of the bedrooms. The stairway, which can be lit via one facade, represents an important spatial element across from the entranceway. The space opening up here serves as a central node for the different floors. An enlarged wellhole and ceiling openings can create a spacious entrance hall and establish spatial relations over several house levels. The housing development in Viken designed by the architectural firm Tegnestuen Vandkunsten shows that this house type is well suited for both semidetached and terraced housing.

This very wide house type is also suitable for homes that are strongly oriented to one side, as in dense back-to-back housing developments; or for homes constructed directly on a noise barrier, like those in the Cyclops project executed by the Dutch architectural office Nio. Here the upper level protrudes and recedes in comb-like fashion to create a longer facade with improved lighting conditions. A glazed ceiling allows light to fall from the first floor into the very dark entrance area (fig. 2.1; 2.19).

Terraced houses with three or more south-facing rooms have a much more spacious effect and bear greater resemblance

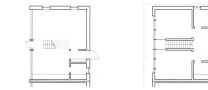
2.18

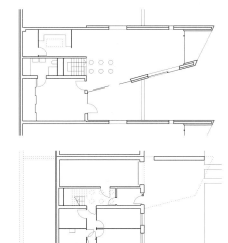
2.19
2.20

2.15 First floor plan, terraced housing development in Munich; von Seidlein
2.16 First floor plan, terraced houses in Darmstadt, 2003/2004; zimmerman. leber.feilberg architekten
2.17 Floor plans, development of semidetached houses in Ostfildern, 2006, Fink + Jocher
2.18 Floor plans, development in Röthenbach an der Pegnitz, 1991; Metron Architekten
2.19 Floor plans, development with noise barrier in Hilversum, 2001; Maurice NIO
2.20 Terraced houses in Stuttgart, 2003; Kohlmayer Oberst Architekten

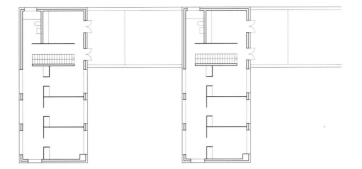

2.21

2.22

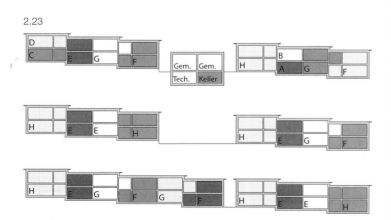

2.23

to detached single-family dwellings. When terraced houses were first developed, a primary goal was to fit as many units as possible into a single row, which resulted in narrow, deep floor plans. However, using the same floor area, architects can significantly improve natural lighting conditions and the quality of living with expanded house width and reduced house depth. This type of design is often avoided, however, because a larger portion of the property runs along public infrastructure (streets, paths, etc.).

L-shaped types

L-shaped and angular floor plans are one way to improve natural lighting conditions on narrow, deep properties. The complex of LBS-Systemhäuser in Neu-Ulm consists solely of L-shaped semidetached and terraced homes. They require the same plot width as two-room-wide houses, yet they feature only one room that extends to public infrastructure. The stairway and building services are located at the central vertex of the angle. Up to three bedrooms can be added on the upper floor, and roof terraces are also possible.

The linked houses designed by Becher + Rottkamp in Berlin were also conceived as L-shaped, terraced dwellings. The stairways and services are located in the vertex of the two wings. Since the two bathrooms, which receive direct sunlight, lie on the exterior facade, the houses are wider than those in Neu-Ulm, benefiting the courtyard, which is large enough for a tree (fig. 2.21).

Complex designs

One characteristic of urban living is the mixture of different groups of residents. In contrast to single-family homes that are individually designed for a single client, planners are increasingly regarding semidetached and terraced housing as products designed and built for different users. One strategy for addressing their different needs is to offer diverse house types [20] instead of providing the same house with a questionable flexibility. Experience shows that this flexibility usually only exists when the house is designed for first-time residents; there are usually never any subsequent modifications. This is possibly one of the reasons why the *"Schaltzimmer"* has increasingly disappeared from the repertoire of terraced house designs in Germany since the mid-1990s. This is a room between two terraced homes that can be used at times by one, at times by the other party. [21] Today architects are increasingly turning to interwined units or combining units of different sizes. At Wohnhaus e.G., a housing cooperative in Weimar, planners and future residents combined eight different-sized house types (small/large planted courtyard, varied number of bedrooms) to form several rows of dwellings (fig. 2.23).

The terraced houses in Kanoya have much more dramatically intertwined designs than those in Weimar. Similar rowed concrete stairways lead up to their first floor, where all the units are equally wide. However, groups of three units intertwine on the top floor to create entirely different spatial structures that one can hardly imagine when viewing the houses from the outside (fig. 2.22).

Another type of asymmetrical design can be seen in the houses in Almere by UN Studio. Each individual house engages its surroundings through projections and recessions. On all sides of the single-family, semidetached and terraced houses, offset spatial modules create spectacular projections over the water, roofed sitting areas, parking spaces, as well as terraces on different levels. The modules and resulting spaces point in different directions, forming many niches and corners to preserve privacy and shield residents from view (fig. 2.26).

As described under the heading "Typologies," there are also interesting complex designs for semidetached houses. The extremely wide twin house in Münchenstein (see p. 112ff.) shows that these designs are not only found in relatively square floor plans. The first unit has a wide ground floor and a narrower upper story. The ground floor of the second unit is narrow but widens on the upper floor, accessible via a cascading stairway. Galleries and ceiling openings dramatically choreograph this expansion of interior space (fig. 2.24).

Three-dimensional spatial relations

The distribution of rooms in a unit across several floors – the norm for semidetached and terraced housing – creates disadvantages for older residents who must negotiate the stairs between the different levels. Yet it is precisely this stairway that can be used, not only as a connecting element, but also to open up space across several levels, as exemplified in the semidetached houses in Münchenstein. An enlarged wellhole can also have a positive effect on the way space is experienced. An entrance area in the interior of a house can be considerably enhanced by a skylight over the stairway (see the terraced houses in München-Harlaching) or by windows in a recessed attic floor that let daylight into the stairwell.

If a house has low ceilings, a spacious hall-like quality can be created by an entrance area or a living room extending over two levels, even if the actual area is small. The contrast between lower and higher spaces is much more impressive if there is a lower ceiling (2.5 meters).

Split-level designs break with floor plans that traditionally stack functional areas on top of each other. In this case, each half of the floor plan is separated by about half a story from the adjacent level and connected to it by a relatively short stairway. The Diagoon houses designed by Hermann Hertzberger in Delft, Holland (1967–71), reveal the three-dimensional potential of the concept. Projections and recessions on the individual levels create open or secluded areas, and the open interior area, extending across all levels and flooded with sunlight from above, forms the spatial and thematic center of the building (fig. 2.25).

Although more complicated to build, split-level floor plans are excellently suited for sloping properties where they can medi-

2.24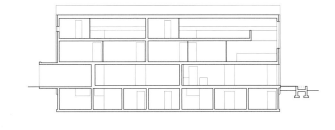

2.25

2.26

2.21 First floor plan, terraced houses in Berlin, 2000; Becher + Rottkamp Architekten
2.22 Ground floor and first floor plan, terraced houses in Kanoya, 2002; NKS architects
2.23 Schematic section, Wohnhaus e. G. Weimar, 1998; Walter Stamm-Teske with Schettler & Wittenberg Architekten
2.24 Longitudinal section, twin house in Münchenstein, 2001; Steinmann & Schmid
2.25 Ground floor and first floor plan, Diagoon houses in Delft, 1971; Hermann Hertzberger
2.26 Groups of houses in Almere, 2001; UN Studio Van Berkel & Bos

2.27

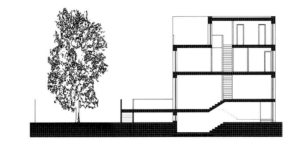

2.28

ate between different site heights. It is advantageous if the difference between the levels is greater or less than half the height of one story – as in the terraced houses in Küsnacht, where the dining area on the upper side of the slope affords a view of the valley through the living room. If the difference between adjacent levels in this building were exactly half the room heights, people sitting at the dining table would only see the edge of the living room ceiling (fig. 2.29).

Closely related to the split-level design are houses in which the rooms on the ground floor respond to the spatial situation with different heights and floor levels. The design for the townhouses in Oberhausen[22] features garages on the lower level directly on the road. The raised ground floor above this is hidden from view from the street. Overlooking the quiet yard is a high-ceilinged room with a slightly raised terrace that offers greater privacy than the shared lawn (fig. 2.28).

Current and future housing needs

The traditional family can no longer serve as the yardstick for marketing homes in the future. The breakdown of family structures, as well as patchwork families and the strong individualization of family members, is changing the way we live together today. Even if today's owners are families in the traditional sense with school-age children when they move into their homes, the demands that these children place on their individual spaces will change in just a few years as they become young adults and use the space more as they would apartment shares. The same applies to multigenerational living arrangements, where older members of the household cohabit with younger people despite their different daily rhythms. And residences shared by different groups (students, working people, retirees) are no longer strictly an urban phenomenon.

We have already mentioned the requirements for well-functioning bedrooms and personal spaces. Entirely different uses are possible if, for example, a narrow, two-story terraced house is laid out to create a kitchen/dining area next to the entrance area and three equally large rooms along the facades. The room on the ground floor can be a shared living area for families, or a bedroom in a house share. If a family has small children, it can accommodate the parents' bedroom, while a louder area for the playroom and children's rooms can be set up upstairs. This layout can change as the children grow older, and the upper area can become a quieter space. Such a flexible concept allows one level to be outfitted with all the necessary functional areas (bedroom, bathroom, kitchen, dining area) for a physically disabled member of the household (either a handicapped or elderly person), even if the barrier-free design is restricted to one level. The flexible concept also permits entirely individualized interior layouts, particularly in terraced homes, without forgoing homogeneous exterior designs that blend in well with urban contexts. As the New Rummelsburg project by the Berlin architects Beyer + Schubert shows, this issue plays an important role in the design and construction of homes where a group of people have joined together to realize their housing dreams. Over thirty units have been built based on the firm's concept for a three-story terraced house with a consistent exterior design. The gabled houses are executed in dark brick, and despite the identical appearance of all units, the individuality of the homes is apparent. Depending on the owners' wishes, diverse floor plans are possible, ranging from an open loft rising four stories to a division into six individual spaces. They are cheaper than freestanding houses due to the joint purchase and shared construction costs (fig. 2.27).

Despite all trends toward greater individualization, architects should always make sure that house layouts have a universal quality. Since houses are often resold and used by other parties, the need for special solutions should be carefully weighed against the advantages of adaptable designs and neutral spatial layouts. If, during the planning phase, houses are offered with different possible layouts, they usually will be easier to remodel afterward (non-bearing interior walls). It is just as important to carefully design the exterior form and individual outdoor areas as it is to integrate the special quality of a location (views, neighborhood, etc.). Most importantly, carefully planned relations to exterior space significantly boost the quality of living. For the most part, these relations can be better managed and designed in high-density house types (terraced houses) or in larger, more compact semidetached houses than in freestanding single-family homes in which everyone can observe everyone else. And it is precisely this use of historical architectural forms such as the villa with a yard and the (urban) terraced development that can provide impetus for future developments in semidetached and terraced housing.

13 Eberhard Wurst, "Innen und außen – der zeitgenössische Wohnungsbau auf der Suche nach dem Besonderen," in *Verdichtetes Wohnen,* edited by Christian Schittich (Munich, 2004), 30.
14 Rüdiger Krisch, "Individuell und nachhaltig," 16.
15 Peter Faller, *Der Wohngrundriss,* 344.
16 Hannes Weeber and Simone Bosch, *Nachhaltig gute Wohnqualität* (Stuttgart, 2004), 63.
17 In a survey of the residents of nineteen housing developments carried out in conjunction with the *Nachhaltig gute Wohnqualität* study, 84 percent said that daylight was important. See Hannes Weeber und Simone Bosch, *Nachhaltig gute Wohnqualität,* 64.
18 Frank-Berthold Raith, Lars Hertelt, and Rob van Gool, *Inszenierte Architektur,* 72ff.
19 See Walter Stamm-Teske, *Preiswerter Wohnungsbau: 1990–1996; eine Projektauswahl Deutschland* (Düsseldorf, 1996), 50ff.
20 Frank Kaltenbach addresses this topic in relation to the construction of large apartments in his editorial "Wohnen heute – Vielfalt statt Flexibilität," *Detail* 3/2006.
21 See Walter Stamm-Teske, *Preiswerter Wohnungsbau,* 30ff.: Ingolstadt, Kellerstraße, Meck & Köppel, and p. 50ff.: Röthenbach an der Pegnitz, Werner-von-Siemens-Straße, Metron Architekten.
22 "LBS-Stadthaus – Im Zentrum zuhause" (LBS-Bundesgeschäftsstelle: Berlin, n. d.), 28f.

1 www.immobilienscout24.de
2 www.immobilienscout24.de
3 See Harald Bodenschatz, "Städtebau – Von der Villenkolonie zur Gartenstadt," in *Villa und Eigenheim: Suburbaner Städtebau in Deutschland,* edited by Tilman Harlander (Ludwigsburg, Munich and Stuttgart, 2001), 77.
4 Harald Bodenschatz, " Städtebau," 98f.
5 See "Anmerkungen zur Geschichte des Reihenhausbaus," in Johannes Kottjé, *Doppel- und Reihenhäuser* (Munich, 2004), 7f.
6 See Frank-Berthold Raith, Lars Hertelt, and Rob van Gool, *Inszenierte Architektur: Wohnungsbau jenseits des Standards* (Stuttgart/Munich, 2003), 46ff. (Brandevoort) and 114f. (Slot Haverleij).
7 See Frank-Berthold Raith, Lars Hertelt, and Rob van Gool, *Inszenierte Architektur,* 72ff.
8 See F. K. Meurer, "Rahmenbedingungen," in *Preiswerter Wohnungsbau in den Niederlanden 1993–1998,* edited by Walter Stamm-Teske, Benedikt Sunder-Plassmann, and Indra Kupferschmid (Düsseldorf, 1998), 5ff.; and Rob van Gool, Lars Hertelt, Frank-Berthold Raith, and Leonhard Schenk, *Das niederländische Reihenhaus: Serie und Vielfalt* (Stuttgart/Munich, n.d.), 8ff.
9 Diener & Diener, Karelse Van der Meer, de Architekten Cie., Topos.
10 *Wonen in een huis naar eigen ontwerp op Borneo-eiland* (Stedelijke Woningdienst Amsterdam: Amsterdam, 1999), and Frank-Berthold Raith, Lars Hertelt, and Rob van Gool, *Inszenierte Architektur,* 56ff.
11 *neues bauen am horn: Eine Mustersiedlung in Weimar,* edited by Lars-Christian Uhlig and Walter Stamm-Teske (Weimar, 2005), 72ff.
12 For example, in the section "Nutzung und Bausteine" in Rüdiger Krisch, "Individuell und nachhaltig – zeitgemäße Einfamilienhäuser," in *Einfamilienhäuser,* edited by Christian Schittich (Munich, 2005) 15f; and in "Funktionsverdichtungen im Wohngrundriss" in Peter Faller, *Der Wohngrundriss* (Stuttgart/Munich, 1997), 30ff.

2.27 New Rummelsburg, Berlin, 2004; Beyer + Schubert Architekten
2.28 Section, urban terraced houses in Oberhausen, design, 2005; Klaus Theo Brenner and Walter Stamm-Teske
2.29 Terraced houses in Küsnacht, 1999; Weber Örtli

2.29

Guidelines to Energy-Efficient Building with Special Consideration of Construction of Semidetached and Terraced Houses

Patrick Jung

According to the currently valid definition, "energy-efficient building" refers to the construction of buildings in which the construction process uses a minimum of resources and the buildings themselves consume minimal energy sources in operation while achieving a maximum in interior comfort. In this context, the term *resources* applies not only to building materials, but also to all kinds of fuels.

Reducing energy consumption and increasing living comfort are a timeless guideline, since they are regarded by all sides as positive. Working against this is the additional effort in new construction and also in residential redevelopment, which can nevertheless be kept to a minimum with farsighted and effective planning. When new semidetached or terraced houses are built, the best conditions for saving energy can be achieved with a smart energy plan.

This article will present some concrete examples to show how to build a house with minimal operational energy consumption. A special focus will be placed on the additional options for savings offered by semidetached or terraced houses.

Energy-efficient building will be a subject of long-term topicality and a matter of concern to virtually all builders and owners, not least through the introduction of *building energy certification.* The EU Building Directive (2002/91/EC) of December 2002, which is expected to become national law in Germany starting in 2006, stresses the necessity of conserving resources in construction: with the 2006 amendment to Germany's energy conservation ordinance, anyone intending to sell or issue new leases for any private or commercial property, whether new or existing, must acquire energy certification for that building. Such certification is valid for ten years and must then be renewed.

The energy performance certificate will document the energy requirements for hot water and heating in residential buildings, enabling a comparison. Builders, buyers, and renters will thus have an energy consumption standard that will provide a basis for an ecological evaluation of a building and help determine its market value. The introduction of the energy certificate will allow potential tenants or buyers to get advance information about the energy requirements of the real estate and consider follow-up costs before making a decision. Against the background of rising energy costs, the energy performance certificate can help consumers develop a consciousness for energy-efficient building, similar to the awareness that already exists, for example, regarding

"Energy Class A" appliances and food products with the "Bio" organic seal. Energy certification will document the energy consumption, the importance of which should not be underestimated in real estate marketing.

There are two different types of energy certificates. A distinction is made between consumption certificates and demand certificates. The consumption certificate is drawn up on the basis of empirical use data tailored to local climate conditions for secondary energy for heat and electricity; the more specific demand certificate is drafted on the basis of analytic benchmarks for the primary, secondary, and useful energy required for heat and electricity. Both procedures involve a balancing process with a target-performance analysis. The cost of certification is based on the size of the building and the time and effort needed to collect the relevant data.

It will clearly be less expensive for builders of similar semidetached or terraced houses to obtain energy performance certification than it will be for owners of single-family dwellings. If an evaluation of several identical housing units – making up a twin house, for example – is commissioned, the costs for determining the data important from an energy perspective (and thus the overall expenditures) will be only slightly greater than those for a single-family house, but each residential unit will receive its own energy performance certificate.

From today's perspective there is every indication that buildings that are designed and built with energy efficiency in mind, and that ideally can document their energy advantages in the specific form of an energy performance certificate, will in the future have obvious advantages on the real estate market – regarding both rental and sales.

What does the term "energy-efficient building" mean? A description of the concepts:
Energy-efficient construction aims not only to reduce the energy consumption of a building to a minimum, but above and beyond that to design it to operate in an environmentally sound manner. In these considerations, a distinction is made between primary, secondary, and useful energy. In the building sector there is great potential for savings (up to 90 percent) in all of these energy forms.

3.1 Facade detail with collector element,
Twin house in Bregenz (1996), Walter Unterrainer

Primary energy is energy contained in natural resources or raw materials. All energy sources that are mined or extracted are available only in limited supplies, so we refer to them as nonrenewable primary energy sources. These include petroleum, natural gas, and uranium. Renewable primary energy sources are those which can be replenished indefinitely, that is, their consumption does not deplete a limited supply of natural resources. They include solar energy, biomass, and geothermal energy sources.

The sparing use of nonrenewable – that is, limited – energy sources is a dictate not only of the economy, but also of reason. Resources that are rapidly diminishing must be consumed much more sparingly and slowly, not only to reduce the unforeseeable impact on the atmosphere and climate, but also to avoid distribution struggles between industrial nations and developing economic powers. Such conflicts could ultimately be massive and, in a worst-case scenario, involve war. However, even renewable energies should be used sparingly, since considerable costs are involved in their generation. They can also have a high environmental impact, as impressively documented by the sometimes heated debate on large dam projects, wind parks, and biomass monocultures.

In order to be usable at all, any form of primary energy must first be transformed and delivered to the consumer. Once the energy source is "refined" to such an extent that the customer can buy it, it is referred to as *secondary energy* (heating oil, gas, and electricity). The conversion to secondary energy can be more or less costly depending on the form of energy. Electricity, for example, is produced throughout Europe in a variety of power plants geared toward different, mostly nonrenewable primary energy forms. Taking into consideration losses due to transport and conversion, 2.7 energy units of primary energy are used to produce 1 energy unit of electricity. Regarding heating oil and gas, the primary energy factor of 1.1 is more favorable.

When builders plan their heating systems, they ultimately decide which secondary energy form they will use. With respect to primary energy consumption, the optimal decision would be for a renewable fuel such as pellets, or for connection to a long-distance heating system, which also requires very little primary energy. When building semidetached or terraced houses, builders should consider that although an installation such as a pellet heating system might be expensive to purchase, the cost can be reduced if builders of several houses place a joint order for a large number of systems, thereby paying lower prices; or if several builders share one heating system.

After secondary energy goes through additional "processing" it becomes *useful energy.* Space heating, for example, involves installation of a boiler, a heat distribution system, and a heat-emitting surface. The distribution and emission processes inevitably involve some energy loss. At this point builders can intervene in the planning phase by committing themselves to low consumption and by selecting a building method that is as energy-efficient as possible, such as building semidetached or terraced houses instead of a free-standing single-family dwelling.

Basic considerations regarding energy-efficient building
There are a number of options available for building in an

3.2

■ Single-family house
■ Terraced house
■ Semidetached house

Heating requirements (kWh/m²a)

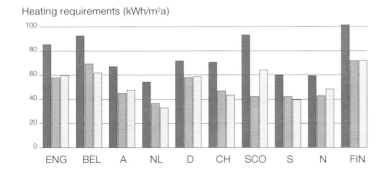

energy-efficient manner. The most obvious approach is certainly to reduce the need for useful energy. This involves keeping heating requirements as low as possible. It can be achieved both by avoiding heat loss and by maximizing heat gain.

Good thermal insulation and high-quality windows help avoid heat loss. A house design aimed primarily at minimizing heat loss would thus have rather small windows, since insulated walls transfer far less heat to the outside than windows and doors do. Many residences built as passive houses, especially early models, are based on this principle. However, a considerable number consequently suffer from a lack of daylight. Such specifications can also seriously limit the spaciousness of the design.

Another option is to maximize heat gain. This option takes advantage of large windows on south-facing walls to achieve a positive balance between nightly heat loss and solar radiation gain. These houses combine the desire for daylight and open architecture with the demands of energy efficiency. However, solar energy gain, especially in winter, is often overestimated, and east- and west-facing windows, or even windows facing north, are sometimes assumed to contribute to the gain. But at our latitudes these directions do not offer sufficient radiation during the heating season. During the summer months, on the other hand, large windows facing east and west can lead to serious overheating problems. So within the framework of a sensible strategy to maximize gain, only south-facing windows should be designed as large as possible, whereas the amount of glass surfaces in the walls facing other directions should be determined by the calculations of the required and desired amount of daylight in the interior, or based on wishes to have a view of the surroundings.

Determining the amount of glazed surfaces that makes sense from an energy standpoint, in order to find a proper balance between overheating in summer and a positive energy balance in winter, is thus a central challenge for an energy-efficient design. Planning has to take into account more than just the orientation of the house; just as important is the shade provided by neighboring buildings, as well as the surrounding landscaping, the building's heat-storing capacity, ventilation, use of the rooms, and urban context. Nomograms developed precisely for this purpose, which show optimal energy solutions for south facades, can help in planning.[1]

In this overall context, the residents of the house ultimately also need to be considered. Good architects and technology can influence the residents' behavior and help them avoid energy loss. User-friendly heat regulators and demand-dependent records of consumption are just two ways to achieve this goal. The proper layout of rooms requiring different temperatures also plays an important role – in other words, the correct zoning of the floor plan. In this respect, a stairway, winter garden, or vestibule can be designed as secondary use zones, for which low interior temperatures in the winter are sufficient, but which at the same time fulfill an important function in protecting against wind, weather, and temperature for the fully heated core zones.

In summary, the following guidelines can be said to minimize the heating demands of a building:

- Minimal exterior surfaces
- Compact building form
- High insulation standards
- Windows on south-facing walls
- Highly insulating window frames and high-quality, energy-saving glazing
- Arrangement of fully heated zones in the building interior, and partially heated or unheated zones at the building periphery.
- Winter gardens, vestibules, and stairwells with a thermic function.

Semidetached and terraced houses offer especially good attributes for energy-efficient building:
- The shared party wall alone is – insofar as it is not the southern wall of a building – a great advantage, since it reduces energy loss and therefore contributes to savings in heating energy. The remaining exterior walls need to be protected from heat loss, primarily through thermal insulation, and in isolated cases through buffer zones such as vestibules and winter gardens.
- Additional options for saving energy are shared installations such as solar collectors on surfaces subject to particularly intense solar radiation. The output for a joint system serves the residents of even those houses or semidetached houses that have a less favorable orientation to the sun. Such concepts sometimes offer the only possibility for energy-efficient planning, particularly regarding property with a difficult shape or location, for example, gaps in urban contexts.
- The cumulative size of the solar collectors can be smaller and they can run more effectively if several families are served by one hot water system.
- By bringing together a number of consumers, expensive systems such as mini-CHP units or wood pellet heating becomes affordable and usable.

Efficient and optimized systems in supplying heat
In view of future security it makes sense to decide to use gas as an energy source. A natural gas connection opens up various possibilities for heating and also offers the option of cooking with gas and saving additional electricity.

The following options with natural gas exist:
- Gas-fired condensing boiler
- Fuel cells
- Zeolith heating units
- Solar condensing boilers
- Gas mini-CHP unit

In a *gas condensing boiler* the energy content of the natural gas is almost completely utilized. The steam that forms during the combustion process condenses inside the device and released as water. In addition to the condensation heat, the heat contained in the steam is also made usable by the heating system. This can result in a 10 to 15 percent increase in the combustion efficiency as compared to boilers with a

3.2   Heating requirements in the countries of Europe. Calculations based on the energy balancing procedure for buildings in accordance with Euro Norm EN 832. This represents a combination of heat sources and heat sinks. As of 2000.
IEA Task 28 working document, Lund University, Department of Construction and Architecture, Johan Smeds

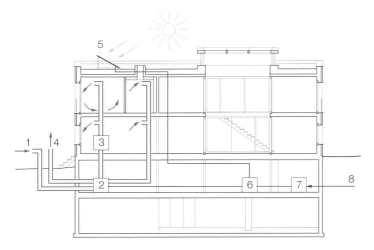

1 Fresh air intake (ground heat exchanger)
2 Heat recovery
3 Air heater
4 Exhaust air
3.3

5 Vacuum tube collectors
6 Solar storage tank
7 Mini-CHP unit
8 Gas connection

3.4

low flow temperature. In order to achieve the greatest efficiency, condensing boilers should be combined with a heating system with a low flow temperature, such as wall, underfloor, or sheet radiator heating units.

In *fuel cells,* atmospheric oxygen and hydrogen bind to a membrane and form water in a controlled process, yielding electricity and heat. The individual cells in which the chemical reaction takes place are connected to achieve the necessary supply voltage and the desired performance. The useful heat in this case is the heat released in the production of electricity. Cooling channels are aligned between the cell packages, in which the heat that develops through reaction losses (30–60%, depending on the process) is discharged and fed into the heat distribution system.
Fuel cell aggregates are connected to the gas and electricity supply. The surplus power fed into the public grid is remunerated by the power authorities. The flue gas is composed largely of steam and is already cooled through the condenser. The demands on the boiler room in terms of space and connections and those on the chimney do not differ significantly from demands on a modern boiler.
Because the chemical energy contained in the fuel is converted directly, stand-by losses are saved and much less maintenance is necessary. These installations also operate silently. The low level of pollutant emissions results from the higher effectivity and mode of operation of the fuel cells, which also means less primary fossil fuels are used. If they are hydrogen based, operations virtually free of emissions are even possible. Fuel cells are on the threshold of marketability. Initial pilot projects with fuel cells have been running successfully, but fuel cell heating is not (yet) profitable due to the low quantities available.

Zeolite heating units are composed of heat storage tanks that are filled and emptied of heat through steam. Zeolites are minerals that are ion exchangers and thus bond easily to water and steam. They release useful heat to the heating unit when water is stored. As the zeolites dry, the heat is stored. The advantage lies in the fact that the heat stored in these units, in contrast to water tanks, does not dissipate over time, but instead undergoes chemical bonding. The heat is generated in the systems presently available by means of gas burners, supported by large solar installations. With an increasing ratio of solar heat, zeolite units are very ecologically sound. It can not be assumed, however, that profitable operation of zeolite heating units will be possible in the near future.

If a solar thermal collector system is already installed, a *solar condensing boiler* should be the heating option of choice. In these devices, the burner and boiler are completely integrated into a hot water storage tank. The gas condensing unit is contained in the upper third of the solar storage tank, so the boiler does not contribute to any heat losses except for those from the flue gas. The construction combines a number of advantages: it is compact, requires only very few connections, produces negligible heat loss, and a high share of the thermal heat comes from solar heat.

A *gas mini-CHP unit* is composed of a gas-fired combustion motor connected to a generator for electricity production and a heat exchanger unit at the cooling water circulation system and at the flue pipe. For semidetached and terraced houses, small gas mini-CHPs are appropriate, which can be designed so that all the lost heat of the small power plant can be utilized as useful heat for space heating and hot water. The electricity produced during operation is either used directly in the house or the costs are covered by utility companies that pay for the power that flows into the public grid. In the last few years a positive development has been observed, since mini-CHP units used to be economical only for large multi-family dwellings or rows of terraced housing. Through the German CHP Act, mini-CHP units have achieved a relevant market share and can therefore be operated economically. Meanwhile there are also some models available that yield good returns in operation in semidetached or single-family homes.

Heating oil as an energy source is facing great cost pressures because of competition from transportation companies and industry. If heating oil is the only available option as an energy source, a condensing boiler should definitely be selected as the boiler type. These systems have improved efficiency because of the low boiler temperatures, low flue gas temperatures, and improved fuel utilization (see gas-fired condensing boilers).
Special types of solar condensing boilers can also be operated using heating oil, and mini-CHP units burning diesel oil or biodiesel are also available.

The environmental significance of *long-distance* heat is based on the degree of flue gas utilization. It is an environmentally sound energy source because it is fed primarily by industrial waste heat in the winter months. In individual long-distance heating systems, fossil fuels are also fired up in the winter, however, in order to cover demand. If there is a high proportion of waste heat, it should definitely be used to heat the service water in the summer.
The regular operating costs of long-distance heat are very high. A long-distance heat transfer station is small and requires little maintenance. A chimney is not necessary and in some cases the connection and equipment costs can also be kept at the almost the same level as those for a conventional boiler.

Wood pellet boiler: Wood pellets are small cylinders of wood shavings, about one-quarter inch in diameter and almost an inch long. The primary supplier for their production is the wood-processing industry. The scrap timber from the sawing industry in Germany alone is sufficient today to heat about 250,000 single-family homes. Only two-thirds of the felling potential in Germany is currently taken advantage of. Within the scope of sustainable forestry, an increase of up to 20 million solid cubic meters (ca. 5.5 million cords) per year would be possible.
Today's pellet boilers are very easy-to-use, fully automatic boilers, comparable with gas or oil boilers. Fully automatic firing and combustion control is standard, as is automatic feed of the pellets into the combustion chamber, cleaning of the flue and heat exchanger, and ash compaction. With combustion procedure control and optimization of the combustion chambers, efficiency ratings of about 90 percent are possible. Complete combustion with low emission values can be achieved using lambda probes, even with a partial load. Use of a buffer storage tank can minimize the number of times it is fired up daily, thereby further improving the effi-

ciency rating and emission behavior. Pellet storage is very simple.
Heat pumps work according to a cycle in which the physical processes of vaporization and condensation are harnessed for heating purposes. They work in a manner similar to a refrigerator, in which heat (corresponding to ambient heat) is removed from the interior and released at a high temperature into the room (corresponding to space heating). The refrigerant used as the cycle fluid does not deplete the ozone layer. However, some refrigerants have a considerable global warming potential if they are released into the environment as a result of leaks or improper waste disposal. The ambient heat used for heating purposes can be taken either from the outside air or the ground (or groundwater). The geothermal type is more efficient and economical in operation, but more expensive to purchase.
When planning a heat pump system, its efficiency, or coefficient of performance (COP), is very significant. A COP of 5 indicates a ratio of 5 Kwh of heat generated from an energy input of 1 Kwh of electricity. Having as high a COP as possible is the prerequisite for efficient and environmentally sound operations. This can be achieved if the temperatures of the heating system and the heat source are as close to each other as possible for instance, if the groundwater as the heat source has a temperature of 10°C (50°F) and the wall or concrete core heating has a flow temperature of 35°C (95°F). Heat pumps are especially good options if a wood heating system is too complex and no gas connection is available. Since a chimney is not necessary, well-planned installations require less maintenance and space than boiler systems. The planning should be carried out carefully by experienced professionals in order to avoid system failure due to a faulty design.

Examples of energy-efficient semidetached and terraced houses
Twin house in Bregenz:[2]
The thermal building behavior was analyzed based on the design plans.[3] Building physics parameters were investigated in order to minimize heating needs. A simulation conducted in the planning phase provided information about the building's thermal behavior and offered prognoses for the space heating requirements and energy balance.
A twin house has a largely symmetrical layout. The special features of this particular design are, first, the use of transparent thermal insulation (TTI), made with a recycled-cardboard, honeycomb construction and a glass curtain wall, and second, the large glazed surfaces on the south-facing facade. The decision to build the innovative corrugated honeycomb cardboard wall was prompted by the fact that the two builders shared the related development costs. The wood–wood fiber–clay composite wall, the Brettstapel ceilings of dowel-joined timber strips, and the full thermal insulation satisfy high ecological demands in the area of construction (see fig. 3.6).

Within the scope of the accompanying computer simulation, the following variations were tested:
· Glazing on the southern facade with a heat transfer coefficient (U) of 1.35 W/m²K, improved to: 0.7 W/m²K

3.3   Example of a mini-CHP system,
      Housing complex in Allschwill, 2004; Amrein Giger Architects
3.4   Housing complex in Allschwill, 2004; Amrein Giger Architects

3.5
Relevant heat transfer coefficient (U) values of the outer shell:

	U-value (W/m²K)
Floor (ground contact)	0.19
Roof	0.16
TTI static*	0.19

* U-value of the TTI wall at night without incident radiation

3.6

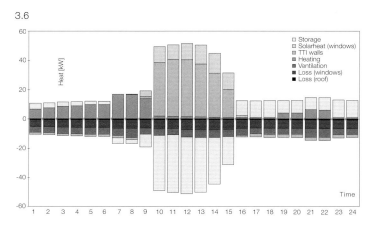

3.7

Time span	Thermic building performance
1:00–7:00 a.m.	At night the building loses heat through heat transmission and ventilation. The losses are compensated for by the heating system and storage tank.
7:00–9:00 a.m.	After the nightly temperature reduction, the room temperature is raised by the heating system, and the cooled-down storage mass is recharged.
9:00 a.m.–4:00 p.m.	The rising sun releases solar heat. This provides heat directly through the windows as well as the TTI walls, by reversing the heat gradient. This clearly shows how large the heat storage capacity is.
4:00–10:00 p.m.	The sun has (nearly) no effect; heat is again taken from the storage tank, and hardly any heating energy is needed. From this point until dawn, the TTI behaves like a conventional insulated wall.
10:00 p.m.–midnight	Nightly temperature reduction starts. As heat is increasingly taken from storage, less energy is supplied by the heating system.

The building performs in a similar manner on overcast days, but there is less fluctuation, especially in the summer months. It should be considered that as statistical climate analyses show temperatures in winter can be expected to be higher on overcast days and nights than on clear days and nights. This is because the cloud cover holds the remaining heat radiation within the atmosphere.

- The TTI wall construction with an additional layer of clay brick on the interior side.

For the simulation, the building was divided into a number of model zones, which made it possible to illustrate the effectiveness of the TTI system. In winter, the incident sunlight penetrates relatively far into the honeycomb structure since the sun's position is rather low. Most of the sunlight is absorbed there and converted to heat. Because of the relatively low thermal conductivity of the honeycomb structure (thermal conductivity = 0.040 W/mK), the temperature within the honeycomb increases, thus reversing the direction of the heat flow: heat losses become heat gains. In contrast, the summer sunlight does not penetrate as deeply into the honeycomb structure. The radiant heat absorbed at the surface of the honeycomb is conducted through the back ventilation.
An exterior blind was planned for use as a sun screen for the south-facade glazing. If the blind is lowered and there is sufficient ventilation, this greatly reduces the solar load and avoids overheating in summer. A wood-fired solid fuel boiler is available to heat the building. Used in combination with a buffer storage tank, it can achieve a steady output of heat, which is very important for a low energy house. Water is heated using solar collectors in the south facade, which are also connected to the buffer storage tank. They round out the overall energy concept for the house.
The thermal behavior of a building can be best described on the basis of the balance of all parameters. Thus the simulation resulted in a series of data for each zone, such as solar heat gain; heat loss through the walls, roofs, and windows; daily temperature variation patterns; dampness; and the necessary performance for heating and cooling (see fig. 3.7).

The simulation of glazing options showed clear advantages of glazing with a heat transfer coefficient of U=0.7 W/m²K instead of 1.3 W/m²K. The transmission heat losses could thereby be reduced by roughly 45 percent. The additional application of clay brick to the fiberboard had virtually no influence at all on energy demand, but it served to make the interior climate more constant and thus more pleasant.
The annual heating energy requirements were simulated for all variants. Since the energy demand hardly varied when constructions had an additional clay brick layer (the values with the clay brick were about 1 percent lower), summer comfort was the most important factor supporting the use of clay brick.
However, different types of glazing on the south-facing facade had an obvious effect on how much heating energy was required. The necessary heating energy could be reduced by about 30 percent by improving the quality of the southern glazing, that is, by using passive-house glazing with a heat transfer coefficient of U=0.7 W/m²K.

With respect to the net floor area (NFA), the following annual energy demand values resulted:
- Using glazing on the south facade with U_{frame} = 1.3 W/m²K: 26 kWh/m²
- Using glazing on the south facade with U_{frame} = 0.7 W/m²K: 19 kWh/m²

"Am Leimbacher Berg" passive house [4]
The design for the "Am Leimbacher Berg" passive house

development won the state competition sponsored by the Ministry for Urban Development and Housing, Culture, and Sports (MSWKS) of the German state of North Rhine-Westphalia. The investor, the GeWoGe housing association (Gesellschaft für Wohnen und Gebäudemanagement), was involved in developing and carrying out the competition from the start.

The project combines the typical characteristics of an efficient passive house with a highly creative design. The passive house is thus presented as a contemporary building form. The residential development features a particularly adept response to the existing urban context and topographical conditions. The building design, which optimizes solar gain, could be successfully implemented because of the particular sloping terrain on parts of the property. The basin-like parts of the property with minimal solar options remained unimproved, but as an open area they present a significant ecological and creative contribution to the design.

Based on a compact, two-story, basic wooden module with approximately 105 sq.m. (1,130 sq.ft) of living space, this type of terraced housing can be extended by about 30 or 55 sq.m. (325 or 590 sq.ft) by adding a recessed top floor or a side extension. The ecological, energy-efficient approach is continued in a consistent manner by using building materials that support healthy living. Thermal insulation with cellulose fiber and OSB wood panels (oriented strand board) are utilized as structural and load-bearing building materials. A glass sunspace extending the entire height of the south facade increases the quality of living and helps shorten the heating period. Together with an efficient window ventilation system in the sunspace, fixed shading structures such as roof and balcony elements prevent overheating in summer. The alignment of the houses makes it possible to achieve an extraordinary compactness. With reference to the volume (V) of the houses, the proportion of heat transmission area (A) is about 40 percent less than that of a scattered arrangement of homes (A/V = 0.6; for single-family dwellings the A/V value is typically 1.0).

The solar housing development is heated with solar and geothermal heat. A heat pump provides hot water and comfortable inside temperatures on cold days. Controlled ventilation of the living space by means of efficient heat recovery is part of the passive house energy scheme. This recovers 90 percent of the heat from space heating, improves the air quality, and prevents mold formation. The air supply and exhaust unit is connected to a 20-meter long geothermal ground loop in order to allow the heat exchanger to operate without freezing. If the air intake draws the ambient air through the pipe laid underground in the yard, the air is preheated in the winter from -10 °C to 5 °C (15 °F to over 40 °F). In the summer, the underground pipe can slightly cool the fresh air down to 22 °C. (72 °F).

Solar collectors can heat the hot water for about 60 percent of the year. They are installed in such a way that they shade the south-facing windows in the summer.

Per housing unit, the collector surface area of the solar instal-

3.8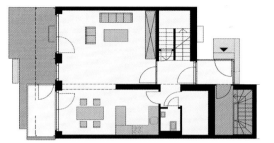

3.9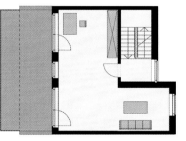

3.10

3.11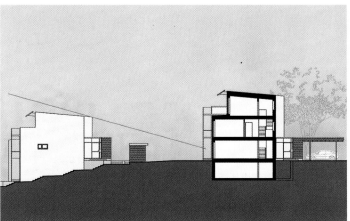

3.5   Twin house in Bregenz, 1996, Walter Unterrainer
3.6   Relevant U-values, Twin house in Bregenz, 1996, Walter Unterrainer
3.7   Thermic building performance, Twin house in Bregenz, 1996, Walter Unterrainer
3.8–3.10 Ground floor and two upper floors, Am Leimbacher Berg passive house complex, Leverkusen, 2005; tr.architekten, rössing + tilicke
3.11   Cross section, Am Leimbacher Berg passive house complex, Leverkusen, 2005; tr.architekten, rössing + tilicke

3.12

3.13

Technical data:

Piping:	PVC
Total length:	45.85 meters
Pipe diameter, inside:	48 cm
Pipe wall thickness:	1 cm
Flow rate, ventilation system:	max. 2000 m³/h
Bedding material:	gravel
Covering:	recycled concrete materials, 40 cm humus
Level:	2.5 m below grade
Groundwater depth:	5 m below grade
Groundwater temperature:	winter 10.9°C, summer 14.9°C sinusoidal characteristic

The simulation model for the ground heat exchanger yielded the following results:

The favorable geological conditions at the site allowed for optimization of the thermal performance of the ground heat exchanger. A temperature gradient of 12 degrees maximum can be achieved at a maximum air flow rate. If the air flow rate is cut to 25 percent, a temperature gradient of up to 20 degrees is achieved. Maximum heat output at midday is 3 kW. Peak outputs of 6 kW are possible under favorable conditions in startup mode. Cooling performance at midday is also 3 kW, with a peak output of 5 kW. The simulation showed that on humid days, the outdoor air humidity in the ground heat exchanger is likely to condense. Under the simulated conditions, a maximum of 30 liters of condensate can be expected. This is collected at the control shaft and released under controlled conditions.
The ground heat exchanger paid for itself in less than eight years, since in this case a very simple system was selected and laid without any additional excavation, and the costs and benefits were equally divided among the nine residential units and one office.

lation is 6.2 sq.m. (66.7 sq.ft); the solar storage tank holds 250 liters (66 gallons) in the compact heat pump device. For reasons of property rights law, each housing unit receives its own ground probe, combined with a main unit for space heating and solar hot water generation. Each system in each housing unit is monitored by its own optimized controller unit, which in this case is significant for the efficiency of the system as a whole.

Ventilation appropriate for a passive house, without reheating, is not automatically regulated, but controlled by the user based on the volume of air needed. This offers a number of advantages:
• It is easy to heat the bathroom.
• There is no unwanted heating of the upstairs rooms due to heating air that rises through the stairwell.
• The temperatures in the individual rooms can be regulated separately.

During planning, it definitely should be assumed that the brine/water heat pump and the solar collector installation both use a single, aligned controller in order to prevent any conflicting signals. The solar heat is given first priority for use. Only when the heat storage tank cools down and no solar yield is available will the heat pump start operation.

The entire energy scheme is based on optimized urban development, in which solar gains in winter are determined through computer simulation. The distances between the houses are calculated so that the winter sun can be used almost completely. Room comfort in winter and summer was also calculated and optimized; the projected, extremely low consumption values of 15kWh/m² per year could actually be achieved in operations. In order to provide the wood structure with lasting protection against moisture damage, precise planning as regards building physics proved necessary, which was verified and thereby documented by an analysis of thermal bridges.

Sagedergasse, Vienna[5]
The exemplary urban housing project built for the Altmannsdorf-Hetzendorf housing association in Vienna won the Austrian Residential Housing Design Prize with more points than had ever been received up to that time. Architect Georg W. Reinberg designed the building and planned the construction on a long, narrow building gap in the center of Vienna's 12th district (Meidling) near Schönbrunn Palace. The site is squeezed between high rises and scattered individual buildings. The east-west orientation of the property offered unfavorable conditions for the use of daylight and solar energy. Although only a narrow corner of the elongated lot faces south, all nine residential units look out to the sun. Despite the extremely unfavorable urban context, the architect succeeded in creating an attractive living environment that conserves resources.
The four standard sections open up to spacious winter gardens facing south, whereby the slope of the pent roof on the north side of each section strongly reduces the mutual shading of the tall structures. All of the incident solar radiation that falls on the property in the winter can be used directly as passive heat gain through the glazing.
The northernmost section, which completes the row of houses toward the street (Sagedergasse), has an office and

a store, which receive diffuse daylight and maintain a connection to the street environment through the glazed north facade. The high, projecting roof of the building slopes to the south, catching the sun's rays, which would otherwise simply heat up the street asphalt. There are 60 sq.m. of flat plate collectors on the roof, which support the hot water heating for all of the residential units.

The dimensions of the thermal insulation and the quality of the glazing in the winter gardens and in the window installations were optimized through simulation calculations and by receiving bids for different variants in order to determine the most effective insulation values. It was ultimately possible to achieve a low energy standard of roughly 25 kWh/m² per annum.[6]

As needed, residents can use a central air intake and exhaust unit with heat recovery. The outside air is preheated in the winter at least 10 degrees (°C) in an underground pipe, and in the summer it is slightly cooled before entering the rooms. The climate-regulating effect of this geothermal measure was verified in advance in a building simulation. Fifty meters of pipe were laid underground within the building pit along the eastern side of the basement row. The costs were minimized by laying the pipe near the outer perimeter of the building, since no significant additional excavation was then necessary. Ever since tenants moved into the housing in spring 1999, they have confirmed the efficient interaction of the underground pipes, ventilation system, heating, and structural engineering. The favorable values calculated in the simulation have even been surpassed in practice (see fig. 3.13).[7]

Conclusions for the planning of semidetached and terraced housing

In order to design energy-efficient residential housing, certain basic architectural considerations are necessary, which optimize use of the potential of solar radiation on a piece of property. An orientation facing the sun constitutes the basis for optimal use of solar heat gain. In this context, terraced houses have a lower probability of mutual shading than scattered single-family homes. On pieces of property with an unfavorable shape and location, terracing houses can also be beneficial since part of the energy gained from the solar collectors on the houses with a favorable orientation can be used for those houses positioned less favorably.

Semidetached or terraced houses can also offer additional advantages due to their compact construction. First and foremost, they avoid heat loss through the reduction of exterior walls. Based on the volume of the building, the exterior surface area in a terraced unit is far less than, for example, in single-family dwellings.

Not until the building shell satisfies the aforementioned conditions for savings and heat gain can the next step be considered, that of selecting the proper heating system. Timely and expert consultation is important here, starting in the early planning phase, since the conditions for taking advantage of ambient heat or conventional energy types vary depending on the location. For example, builders should examine whether a groundwater-source heat pump can be used or if the conditions favor a wood pellet heating system. Semidetached or terraced houses offer the option of lowering costs by sharing a central heating unit, so the savings can be invested in an ecologically sound heating system that is safe for the future.

Notes
[1] See Renate Hammer and Patrick Jung, Beton in der Solararchitektur; download: <http://www.jung-ingenieure.de/>
[2] Design: Walter Unterrainer
[3] using thermal analysis software (TAS)
[4] Design: tr-architekten, rössing + tilicke
[5] Design: Georg W. Reinberg
[6] The heating energy standard in 1999 was 100 kWh/m² per annum. The 2006 standard is 80 kWh/m² per annum.
[7] The dynamic building and plant simulation tool (TAS) from the British company Environmental Design Solutions Ltd (EDSL) was used to perform the simulations. Vienna weather data were taken from a complete series of measurements from 1993.

3.12 Aerial photograph, Sagedergasse housing complex, Vienna, 1998; Reinberg architectural office
3.13 Technical data, Ground heat exchanger, Sagedergasse housing complex, Vienna, 1998; Reinberg architectural office
3.14 Interior, Sagedergasse housing complex, Vienna, 1998; Reinberg architectural office

3.14

Table of projects according to materials used

Timber

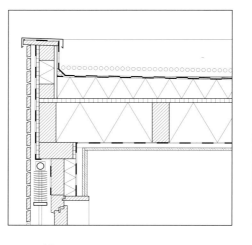

Steel

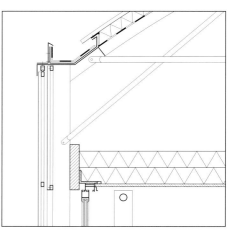

Concrete

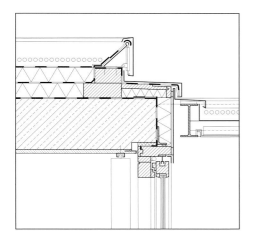

Brickwork and stone

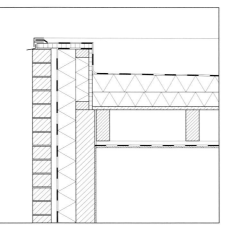

Housing Development in Gantschier

Architect: Hans Hohenfellner, Feldkirch

These timber construction terrace houses are sited on the wide valley floor in Gantschier, in the region of Montafon in Vorarlberg. Forming a compact tract, they offer an alternative to the neighouring free-standing single-family houses with their density of form, and economical and energy-conscious utilization of the site. The elongated row is made up of six two-storey terrace houses measuring 103 m² each.

From the north-eastern approach, the houses appear closed and introverted while the south-west elevation opens up with large-format glazing, balconies and terraces. Passageways cutting through the building provide each individual house with a private access zone, open storage space and a protected terrace, all in one. The ground floor is given over to an open cooking, dining and living area. The first floor, accessed via a single-flight stair, is comprised of the bathroom, three bedrooms and an internal storage room. Planning flexibility is ensured by the utilisation of non-load-bearing partition walling. The structure's dense, prefabricated panel construction system and highly insulated flat roofs comply with the Austrian "eco-standard 1". A central heating system utilizing wood pellets and providing 26 kW of energy, together with 50 m² of solar collectors and large buffer storage, supplies the entire development with sufficient hot water and heating.

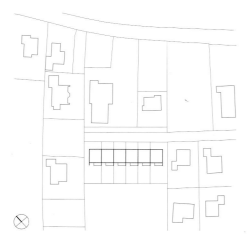

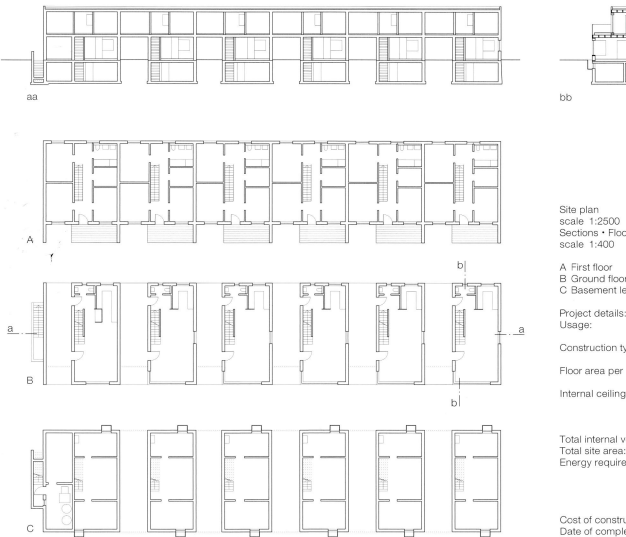

aa

bb

A

a · · a

B

b|

b|

C

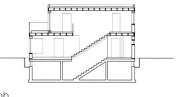

Site plan
scale 1:2500
Sections · Floor plans
scale 1:400

A First floor
B Ground floor
C Basement levelr

Project details:

Usage:	6 terrace houses
Construction type:	timber panel system
Floor area per house:	6x 103 m²
	619.56 m²
Internal ceiling height:	2.39 m (ground floor)
	2.34 m (first floor)
Total internal volume:	2,272 m³
Total site area:	1,572 m²
Energy requirement for heating:	
	70.5 kWh/m²a (end house)
	65.1 kWh/m²a (middle house)
Cost of construction:	1.32 million €
Date of completion:	Summer 2005

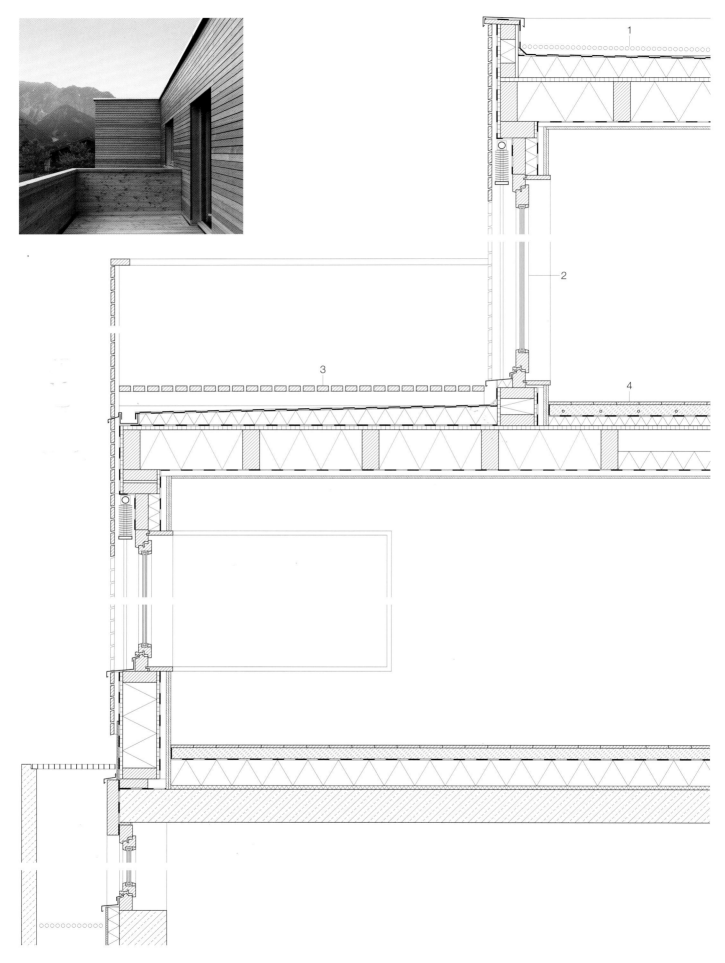

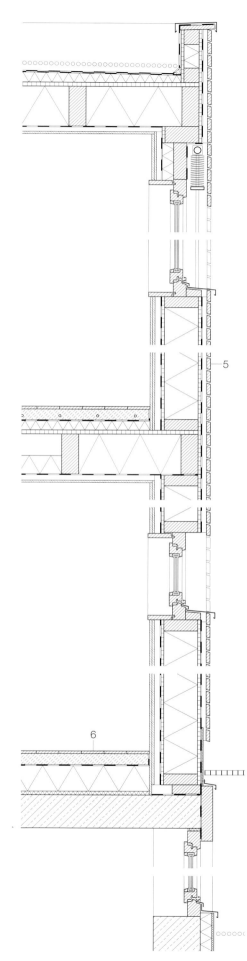

Section   scale 1:20
1 roof construction:
   50 mm gravel, three-ply bituminous sheeting
   separation layer, 40–120 mm insulation, with
   gradient, 22 mm oriented-strand board
   thermal insulation between
   90 × 220 mm timber beams, vapour barrier
   30 mm battens,
   12.5 mm plasterboard
2 larch window frame with double glazing
3 terrace floor construction:
   30 mm larch grid, 80 mm sub-construction
   bituminous rubber membrane
   separation layer, 60–100 mm insulation, with
   gradient, impermeable membrane
   22 mm oriented-strand board
   thermal insulation between
   90 × 220 mm timber beams, vapour barrier
   30 mm battens, 12.5 mm plasterboard

4 first floor construction:
   15 mm parquet flooring, 60 mm screed
   vapour barrier, 50 mm impact-sound insulation
   22 mm oriented-strand board
   thermal insulation between
   90 × 220 mm timber beams, vapour barrier
   30 mm battens, 12.5 mm plasterboard
5 20 × 60 mm larch rhombus boarding
   24 mm ventilation cavity, vapour barrier
   16 mm timber fibreboard, 180 mm insulated
   timber panel, 15 mm oriented-strand board
   vapour barrier, 30 mm battens
   2 × 12.5 mm plasterboard
6 ground floor construction:
   15 mm parquet flooring
   60 mm screed, vapour barrier
   140 mm thermal insulation
   20 mm impact-sound insulation
   180 mm reinforced concrete slab

Terraced Housing in Innsbruck

Architects: Holz Box Tirol, Innsbruck

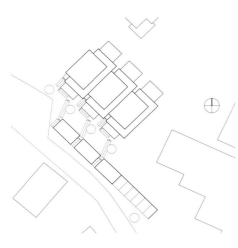

Site plan
scale 1:1000
Sections · Floor plans
scale 1:400

1 Garage
2 Terrace
3 Bedroom
4 Bathroom/WC
5 Living room
6 Dining room
7 Kitchen

The steeply sloping site of this development is located on the outskirts of Innsbruck with views over the Inn Valley and the surrounding mountains. The three tower-like houses dramatically step down the northern slope of the site – the site actually falls away in two directions. Numerous terraces and balconies enlarge the available external space, normally limited on steep sites, by providing direct access to the outdoors from most rooms. A further result of the gradient of the site is that access to the houses has been achieved at two different levels. The individual, cubic forms of the houses are separated and articulated by the recessed entrances and the staircase zones behind.

The structure consists predominantly of prefabricated timber-stud elements with larch cladding; only the northern walls of the stairwells and building elements in direct contact with the ground are constructed of concrete. Enhanced flexibility of the floor layout was obtained by the introduction of steel beams supporting the timber structure; each storey offers open floor plans and allows for individual interpretation of the available spaces. The bedrooms are on the second level of the houses, while the third level, which is surrounded on three sides by a generous roof terrace, is given over to living, dining and cooking activities. Additional light penetrates to the upper levels and internally located rooms through the staircases, which are fully glazed, even transparent in the living areas. Due to the skilful arrangement of entrances and terraces, the three families are able to enjoy an admirable degree of privacy despite the relatively high density of the development.

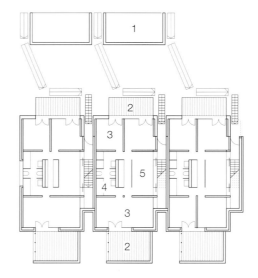

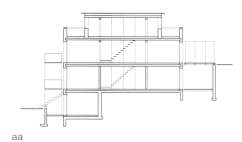

aa

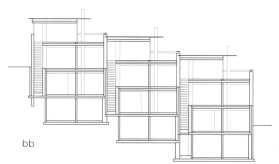

bb

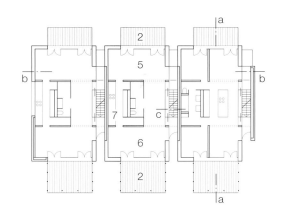

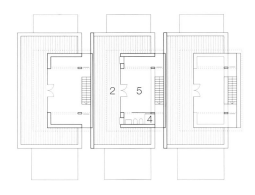

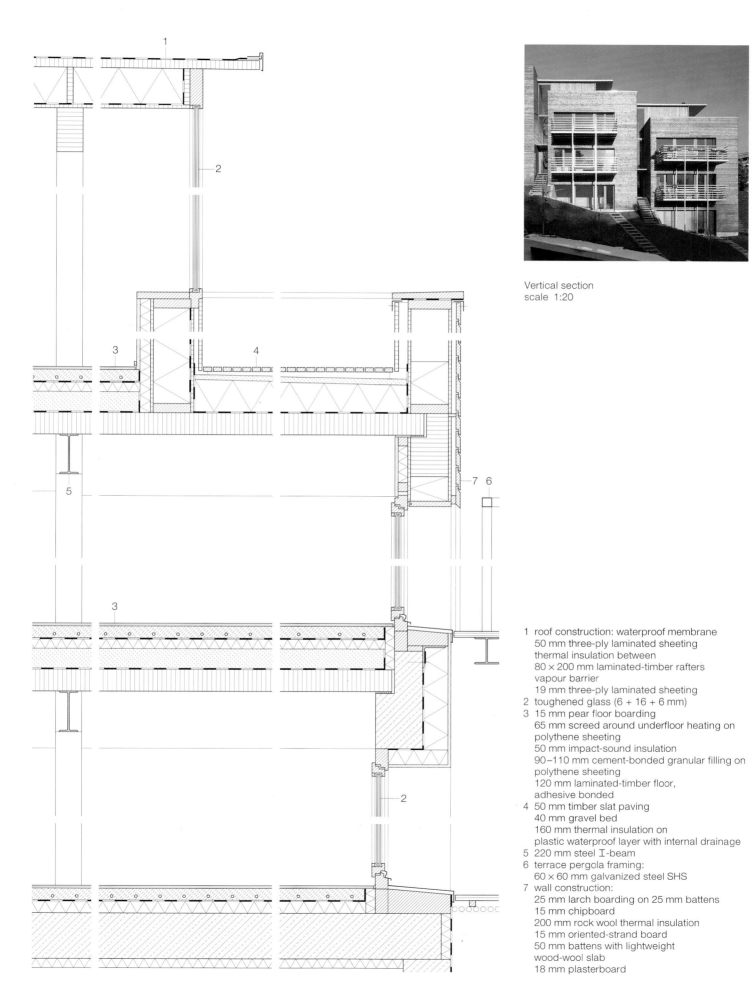

Vertical section
scale 1:20

1 roof construction: waterproof membrane
   50 mm three-ply laminated sheeting
   thermal insulation between
   80 × 200 mm laminated-timber rafters
   vapour barrier
   19 mm three-ply laminated sheeting
2 toughened glass (6 + 16 + 6 mm)
3 15 mm pear floor boarding
   65 mm screed around underfloor heating on
   polythene sheeting
   50 mm impact-sound insulation
   90−110 mm cement-bonded granular filling on
   polythene sheeting
   120 mm laminated-timber floor,
   adhesive bonded
4 50 mm timber slat paving
   40 mm gravel bed
   160 mm thermal insulation on
   plastic waterproof layer with internal drainage
5 220 mm steel I-beam
6 terrace pergola framing:
   60 × 60 mm galvanized steel SHS
7 wall construction:
   25 mm larch boarding on 25 mm battens
   15 mm chipboard
   200 mm rock wool thermal insulation
   15 mm oriented-strand board
   50 mm battens with lightweight
   wood-wool slab
   18 mm plasterboard

47

Project details:
Usage: 3 terrace houses
Floor areas: 2x 150 m²
                      1x 200 m²
Construction type: prefabricated timber-
                      frame construction
Internal ceiling height: 2.5 m
Total floor area: 820 m²
Total internal volume: 2,400 m³
Total site area: 1,080 m²
Energy requirement for heating:
                      49 kWh/m²a
Construction cost: not available
Date of completion: July 1999

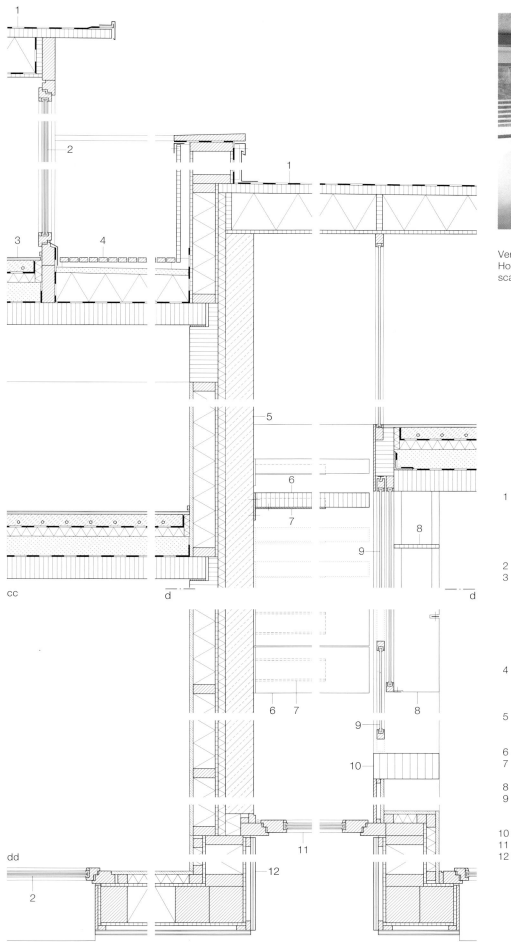

Vertical section
Horizontal section
scale 1:20

cc

d

d

dd

1 roof construction: waterproof membrane
50 mm three-ply laminated sheeting
thermal insulation between
80 × 200 mm laminated-timber rafters
vapour barrier
19 mm three-ply laminated sheeting
2 toughened glass (6 + 16 + 6 mm)
3 15 mm pear floor boarding
65 mm screed around underfloor heating on
polythene sheeting
50 mm impact-sound insulation
90 – 110 mm cement-bonded granular filling
on polythene sheeting
120 mm laminated-timber floor,
adhesive bonded
4 50 mm timber slat paving
40 mm gravel bed
160 mm thermal insulation on
plastic waterproof layer with internal drainage
5 150 mm reinforced concrete wall
30 mm thermal insulation
150 mm timber stud wall with insulation
6 250 × 80 mm parallel strand timber step
7 120 mm steel channel
with fire-resistant coating
8 parallel strand timber shelving on steel flats
9 6 mm toughened glass sliding element
in front of
8 mm toughened glass fixed element
10 350 × 140 mm laminated-timber column
11 entrance door
12 wall construction:
25 mm larch boarding on 25 mm battens
15 mm chipboard
200 mm rock wool thermal insulation
15 mm oriented-strand board
50 mm battens with
lightweight wood-wool slab
18 mm plasterboard

49

Housing Development in Viken

Architects: Tegnestuen Vandkunsten, Copenhagen

Situated near Helsingborg in southern Sweden, this housing development is built on the site of a former school and encircles a small park. It is a modern expression of traditional housing type with double-pitched roofs and gable ends. Distinguished by their dark colouring, the buildings border the old town of Viken with its single-storey dwellings and municipal library to the south. The site is shielded from a nearby bypass road by an earth bank to the north.

As a result of their many years of experience in the field of residential construction the architects were able to develop a scheme with a high degree of visual communication and clear, modern concepts which is nevertheless reminiscent of a village. The spacious green surroundings lend this "black" estate a friendly luxurious atmosphere. All dwellings with ground floor entrances also benefit from additional enclosed gardens.

Three roadways meander through the estate from the southern access road; the low-scale format is enhanced by the carport groups and the pedestrian network spread out between the houses. The quantities of public and private space are well balanced, some of the pedestrian paths, in fact, run immediately past full-height ground floor windows.

In addition to one-and-a-half-storey semi-detached houses and single-storey dwellings, there are also double-storey terrace houses. In spite of large volumetric variety, the various dwelling types create a homogeneous urban entity. The extensively glazed oriel windows, at the corners of the houses, open up the interiors ensuring the ingress of daylight and allowing views in from, and out to, the external environment. Double-height rooms enhance the sense of spaciousness.

The houses are constructed of prefabricated, highly insulated timber-frame elements. The restrained surfaces are based on three main material colours: the dark, anthracite cement fibre-board cladding, the zinc roof sheeting and the areas of glazing. The only other coloration is provided by individual timber casements. Black-painted garden enclosures are subtly incorporated into the composition. The coarse gravel pavers and areas of grass form a natural contrast to the clear-cut lines of the buildings.

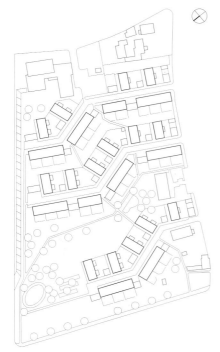

Site plan
scale 1:3000

aa

bb

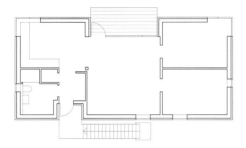

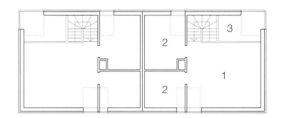

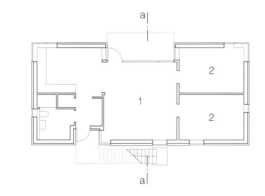

a

A

1

2

2

a

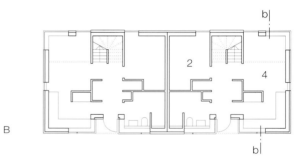

b

B

2

4

b

Sections · Floor plans
scale 1:250

A Single-storey dwellings
B Semi-detached houses
C Terrace houses

1 Living
2 Bedroom
3 Void
4 Dining
5 Shower enclosure

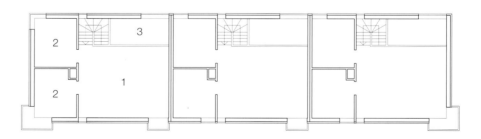

2

3

1

2

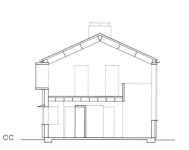

cc

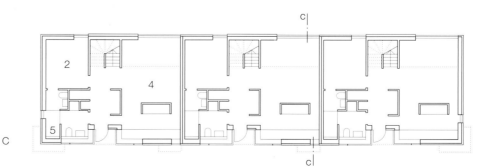

c

C

2

4

5

c

Project details:
Usage: 58 residential units (3 types)
Floor area: 28 type C × 125 m²
                           20 type B × 106 m²
                           5 buildings of 2 type A × 94 m²
Internal ceiling height: 2.4–5.3 m
Construction type: timber-frame construction
Total floor area: 7,000 m²
Total site area: 31,000 m²
Construction cost: 75 million Swedish Kronor
Construction time: Jan 2001 – Apr 2002

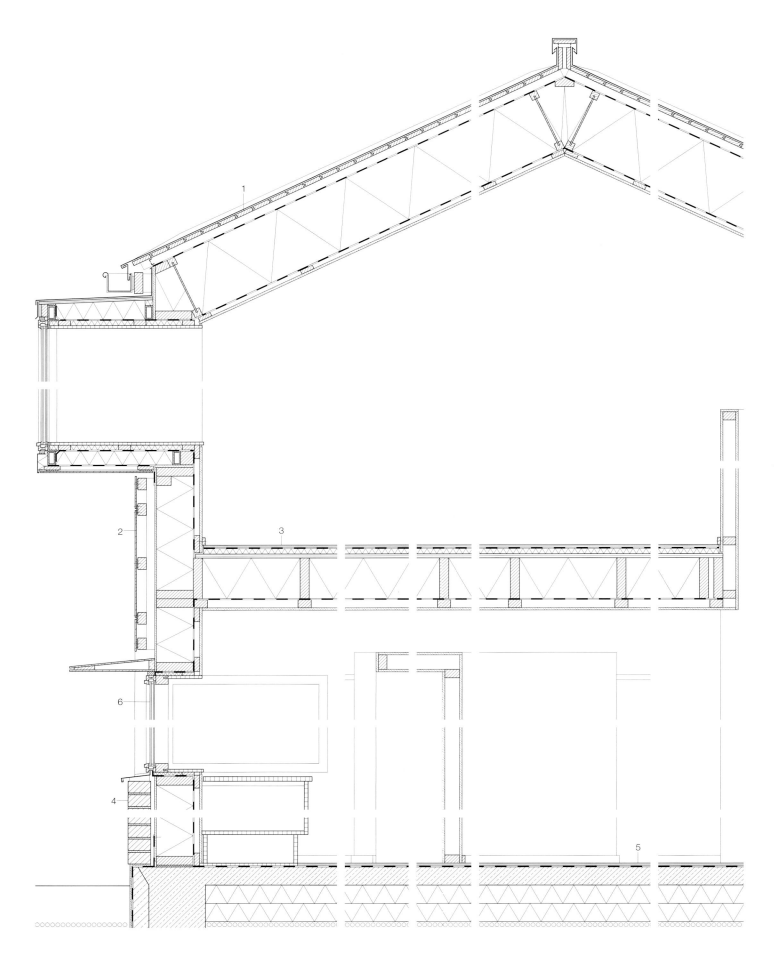

Section   scale 1:20

1 roof construction:
   standing-seam zinc roof sheeting
   impermeable membrane, 22 mm boarding
   45 mm timber element (ventilation cavity)
   vapour barrier
   cellulose-fibre thermal insulation between
   350 mm I-joist purlins (timber flange,
   plywood web)
   0.2 mm polyethylene vapour barrie
   28 × 70 mm battens
   13 mm plasterboard
2 wall construction:
   8 mm cement fibreboard
   45 × 45 mm counterbattens
   45 × 70 mm battens
   9 mm plasterboard
   cellulose-fibre thermal insulation between
   45 × 195 mm timber framing
   vapour barrier
   28 × 70 mm battens
   13 mm plasterboard
3 first floor construction:
   14 mm ash parquet, 2 mm felt
   30 mm impact-sound insulation
   22 mm boarding
   cellulose-fibre thermal insulation between
   45 × 220 mm timber joists
   vapour barrier
   45 × 70 mm battens
   13 mm plasterboard
4 wall construction, ground floor:
   120 mm face brickwork
   30 mm ventilation cavity
   9 mm plasterboard
   cellulose-fibre thermal insulation between
   45 × 195 mm timber framing
   vapour barrier
   28 × 70 mm battens
   13 mm plasterboard
5 ground floor construction:
   14 mm ash parquet, 2 mm felt
   0.2 mm polyethylene membrane
   100 mm reinforced concrete slab
   2 × 100 mm polystyrene thermal insulation
   100 mm gravel drainage layer
6 timber window with double glazing

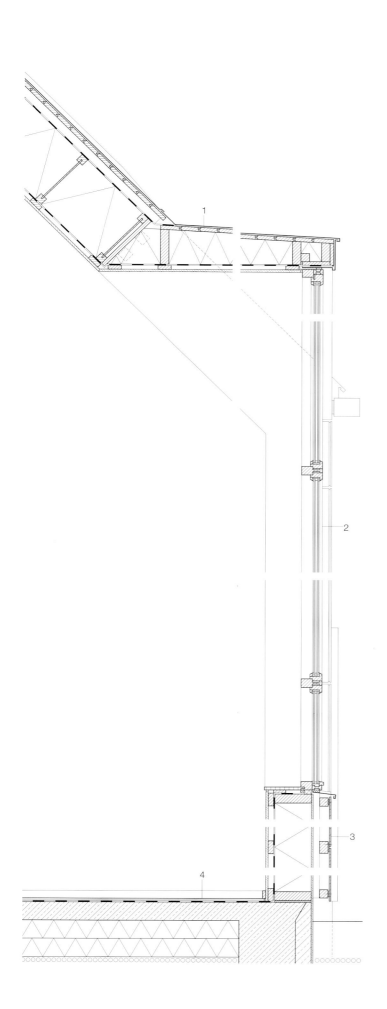

Section   scale 1:20

1 roof construction:
   zinc roof sheeting
   impermeable membrane, 22 mm boarding
   cellulose-fibre thermal insulation between
   45 × 130 – 190 mm timber rafters
   0.2 mm polyethylene membrane
   22 × 70 mm battens
   13 mm plasterboard
2 fixed glazing
   timber window with double glazing
3 wall construction:
   8 mm cement fibreboard
   45 × 45 mm counterbattens
   45 × 70 mm battens
   9 mm plasterboard
   cellulose-fibre thermal insulation between
   45 × 195 mm timber framing
   vapour barrier
   28 × 70 mm battens
   13 mm plasterboard
4 ground floor construction:
   14 mm ash parquet, 2 mm felt
   0.2 mm polyethylene membrane
   100 mm reinforced concrete slab
   2 × 100 mm polystyrene thermal insulation
   100 mm gravel drainage layer

Patchwork House in Müllheim

Architects: Pfeifer Roser Kuhn, Freiburg

Site plan
scale 1:4000

Project details:
Usage: semi-detached houses
Total floor area: 304 m²
Internal ceiling height   2.22–2.77 m
Total internal volume: 1,329 m³
Construction type: timber construction
                              panels, masonry,
                              thermally activated
                              reinforced concrete
Total site area: 804 m²
Energy requirement for heating:
                              77.38 kWh/m²a
Construction cost: 1,579 €/m²
                              480,000 €
Date of completion: April 2005

Semi-detached houses clad in plastic panels tend to stand out from the more conventional constructions in this newly built residential neighbourhood on the edge of Müllheim in Mark-gräflerland. The translucent, reflective external skin creates a fascinating interplay between mirrored images of the land-scape, semi-concealed timber facade panels and shimmering interiors.

The building envelope represents the efficient, yet simple, solar heating concept of the construction and simultaneously contrasts with the more traditional rendered facades of the surroundings. Sheltered under a conventional pitched roof, the complex internal organisation produces an unusual and highly flexible type of house. Two interlocked dwellings are spread over three levels and accessed via a central hall. The floor plan of each dwelling is rotated 90° at each level, ensuring that the residents of both houses receive the benefits of sun and shade in all directions. The living spaces are found on the ground floor, while the bedrooms and bathrooms are located opposite each other on the first floor. The roof level accommo-dates additional recreational spaces, which are once again turned 90° in relation to the first floor plan. The different levels of each dwelling are connected via two opposing staircases located in the central atrium space.

Large-format, light-dispersing, multi-skin facade panels of polycarbonate sheeting form the external envelope; with a U-value of 1.15 W/m²K they make additional insulation mea-sures unnecessary. This material is much lighter than glass and significantly more resistant to hail storms. Sunlight pene-trates the translucent panels causing the central hall to act as a giant solar collector, warming the building from within. Six manually adjustable skylights mounted near the ridge allow for basic temperature control by being opened in summer and closed in winter. On the other hand, solid timber construction elements are located behind the polycarbonate panels in the eaves and within the plane of the roof. The resultant eight-centimetre-wide space acts as a ventilation cavity allowing the naturally warmed air to circulate upwards. Simply constructed reaction flaps built into the foundation of the houses open automatically as a result of the negative pressure, allowing fresh air to enter the building. The warm air is redirected by a fan back down into the lower spaces via a chimney flue. Aerated concrete gable walls provide both sufficient thermal storage mass and thermal insulation. The heating is further supported by thermal activation of the concrete slabs.

Sections (energy concept)
Floor plans
scale 1:250

A Ground floor
B First floor
C Roof level

1 Hall
2 Kitchen
3 Living
4 Bedroom
5 Services/storage
6 Bathroom
7 Gallery
8 Void

aa Ventilation in summer

bb Thermal transfer in winter

cc Thermal transfer in winter

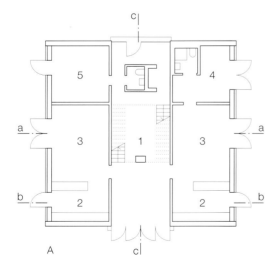

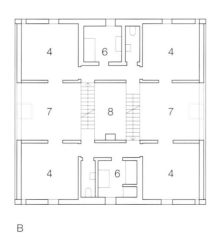

A

B

C

60

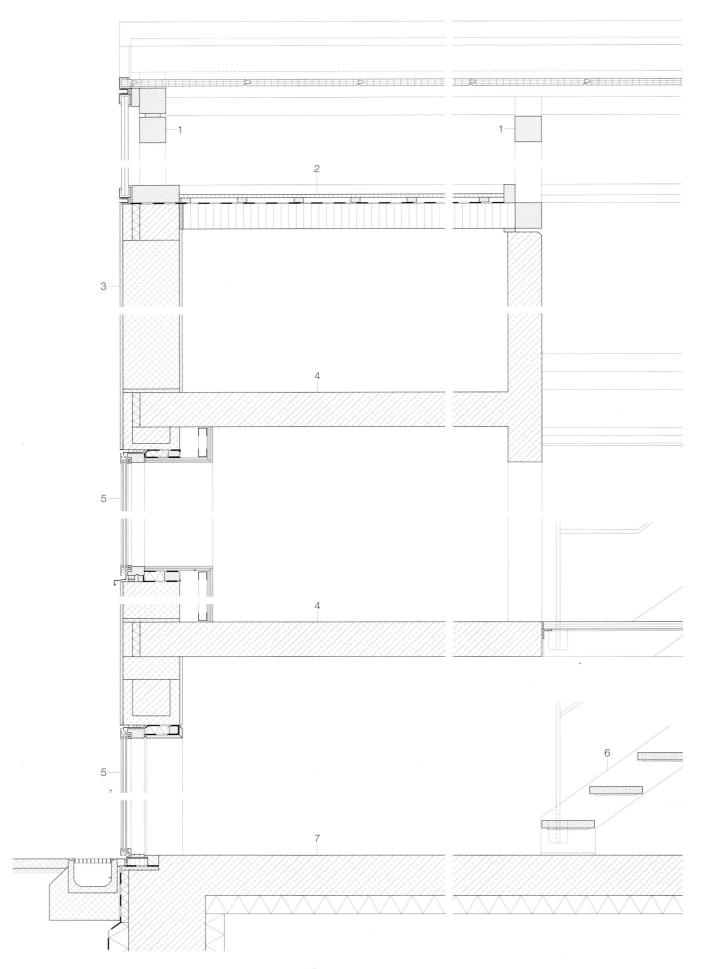

Vertical section gable facade
Horizontal section gable facade
Ventilation collector
scale 1:20

1 140 × 140 mm purlin
2 ridge construction:
   18 mm oriented-strand board
   30 × 50 mm battens
   vapour barrier
   140 mm laminated-timber slab
3 wall construction, rendered
   facade:
   15 mm external render
   624 × 300 × 249 m
   block aerated concrete
   15 mm gypsum render
4 upper floor construction:
   190 mm reinforced concrete

slab, thermally activated
5 timber-aluminium combination
   window with double glazing
6 stair construction:
   40 × 280 mm beech treads
   10 × 200 mm flat steel stringboard
7 ground floor construction:
   220 mm reinforced concrete slab,
   thermally activated
   100 mm polystyrene thermal
   insulation
8 wall construction, ventilation
   collector:
   40 mm polycarbonate multi-skin
   sheeting, mounted on purlin clips
   2 layers 60 × 80 mm battens
   140 mm laminated-timber wall
   panel, vapour barrier
   12.5 mm plasterboard

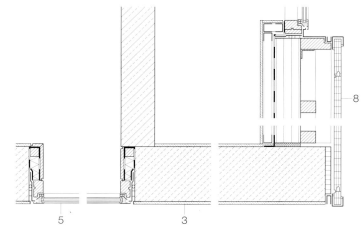

5   3

Vertical sections
Living space · Atrium
scale 1:20

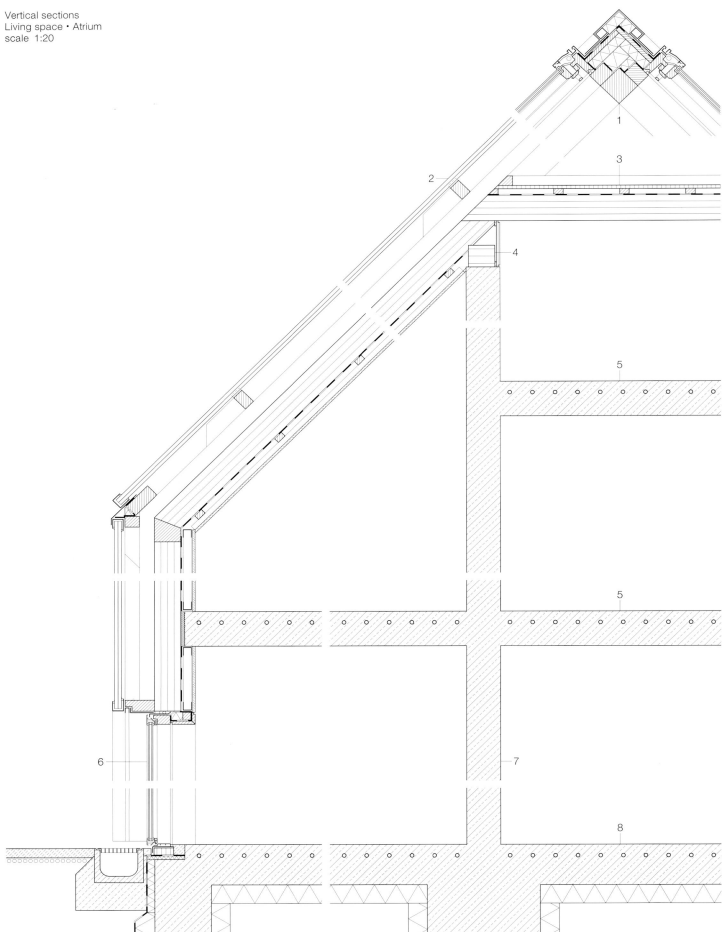

1

3

2

4

5

5

6

7

8

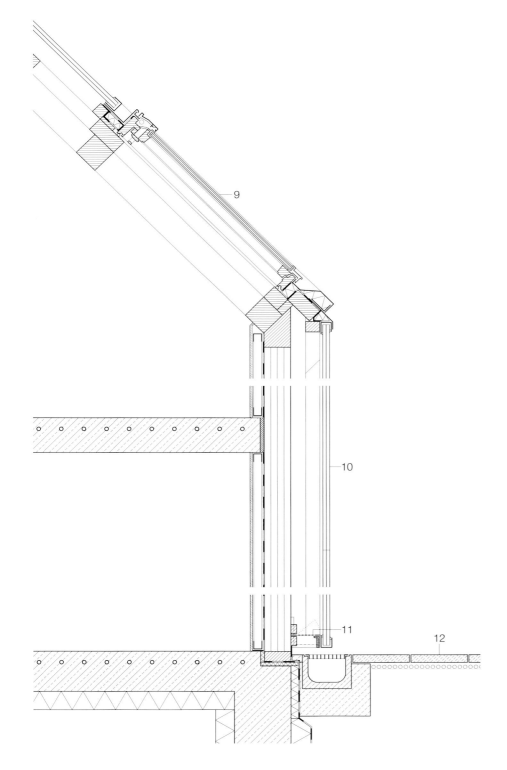

1 140 × 140 mm purlin
2 roof construction, ventilation collector:
   40 mm polycarbonate multi-skin sheeting
   mounted on purlin clips
   2 layers 60 × 80 mm battens
   140 mm laminated-timber roof panel
   vapour barrier
   2 layers 30 × 50 mm battens
   12.5 mm plasterboard
3 ridge construction:
   18 mm oriented-strand board
   30 × 50 mm battens
   vapour barrier
   140 mm laminated-timber slab
4 120 × 140 mm laminated-timber beam
   support
5 upper floor construction:
   190 mm reinforced concrete slab,
   thermally activated
6 timber-aluminium French window
   with double glazing
7 internal wall construction:
   180 mm reinforced concrete
8 ground floor construction:
   220 mm reinforced concrete slab,
   thermally activated
   100 mm polystyrene perimeter insulation
9 576 × 1368 mm hinged roof window
10 external wall construction, ventilation
   collector:
   40 mm polycarbonate multi-skin sheeting
   mounted on purlin clips
   2 layers 60 × 80 mm battens
   140 mm laminated-timber roof panel
   vapour barrier
   30 × 50 mm battens
   12.5 mm plasterboard
11 PTFE membrane reaction flaps
   stainless-steel insect screen
12 terrace construction:
   50 mm mineral-concrete terrace pavers
   on 150 mm granite gravel bed

Terraced Housing in Darmstadt

Architects: zimmermann.leber.feilberg architects, Darmstadt

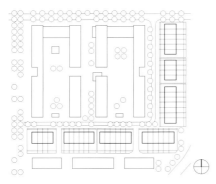

Site plan
scale 1:4000

Project details 1st building stage:
Usage: 22 terrace houses
Floor area: 3x type a (5.0 m)
                        112–122 m²
                        13x type b (5.5 m)
                        124–150 m²
                        6x type c (6.0 m)
                        136–173 m²
Construction type: solid timber construction
Internal ceiling height: 2.40 m/2.75 m
Total floor area: 3,450 m²
Total internal volume: 14,800 m³
Total site area: 6,042 m²
Energy requirement for heating:
                        51 kWh/m²a
Construction cost: 4.5 million €, 918 €/m²
Date of completion: June 2003

Project details 2nd building stage:
Usage: 7 terrace houses
Floor area: 3x type d (without studio)
                        138 m²
                        4x type e (with studio)
                        168 m²
Construction type: solid timber construction
Internal ceiling height: 2.41 m/2.76 m
Total floor area: 1,128 m²
Total internal volume: 5,133 m³
Total site area: 1,343 m²
Energy requirement for heating:
                        45 kWh/m²a
Construction cost: 1.6 million €, 1,000 €/m²
Date of completion: August 2004

K6, a new residential quarter, has been constructed in Kranich-stein on the outskirts of Darmstadt. The architects planned the scheme in such a way as to define the boundaries of the existing urban fabric to the south and to the east in two separate building stages. The southern boundary is made up of four housing blocks of four to six dwellings each, while on the eastern side only the first of three planned blocks is completed with seven dwellings.

All dwellings are privately financed by a community of owners. Guided and advised by the architects, the owners could incorporate their personal wishes at all times during the building process. The narrow houses were restricted to building widths of five to six metres. Nevertheless, it was possible to create generous spatial arrangements through the various combinations of houses, perimeter walling, pergolas and other ancillary structures. Simultaneously, private retreats and outdoor zones were also established. Internal access areas were minimized by locating the kitchen, bathroom and staircase in the centre of the dwellings. The clients were able to choose between various widths for their individual houses; additional roof studios and full or half-basement levels were options, as well. As a result of this, house sizes varied from 112 to 173 m² in the first building stage, and from 138 to 168 m² in the second. The north-south oriented houses, in the first building stage, are protected from the sun on the southern facade by sliding, hinged elements; the floor slabs and partition walls protrude out from the buildings to provide extra sun-shading, simultaneously creating sheltered outdoor terraces and balconies. The east-west oriented houses in the second building stage also benefit from additional outdoor areas created by the balconies, which cantilever out from the first floor and are clad on three sides with timber louvers.

The carcass structure is manufactured entirely of prefabricated solid timber construction panels. This allowed the individual housing units to be assembled on site within one or two days. Together with the precise detailing of the solid timber panels, this construction system ensured an economical and holistic concept. The secondary building elements – roof studios, balconies and other ancillary constructions – are all clad with untreated larch boarding. The primary structures, contrastingly, are clad with reddish three-ply panels or, in the latter building stage, rendered white. This alternation between timber and white render, between projection and recession, and the zoning of the outdoor spaces by walling and other structures, all combine to create the charm of this highly individual terraced housing scheme.

1st building stage A
Section · Floor plans
scale 1:250

2nd building stage B
Section · Floor plans
scale 1:250

1 Entrance
2 Kitchen
3 Dining
4 Living
5 Bedroom
6 Bathroom
7 Studio

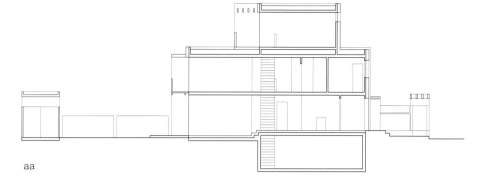

aa

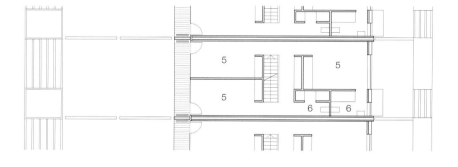

7

5   5
5
6   6

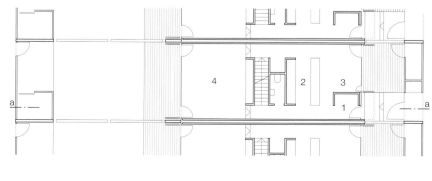

a

4   2   3
1

a

A

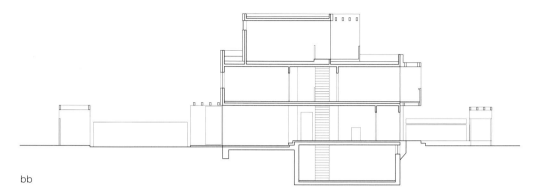

bb

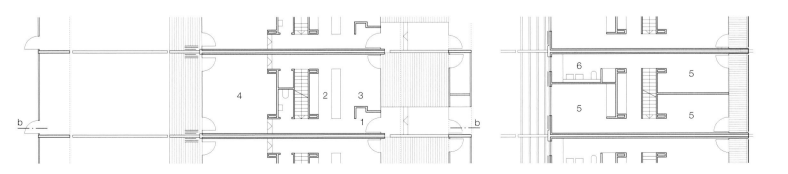

B

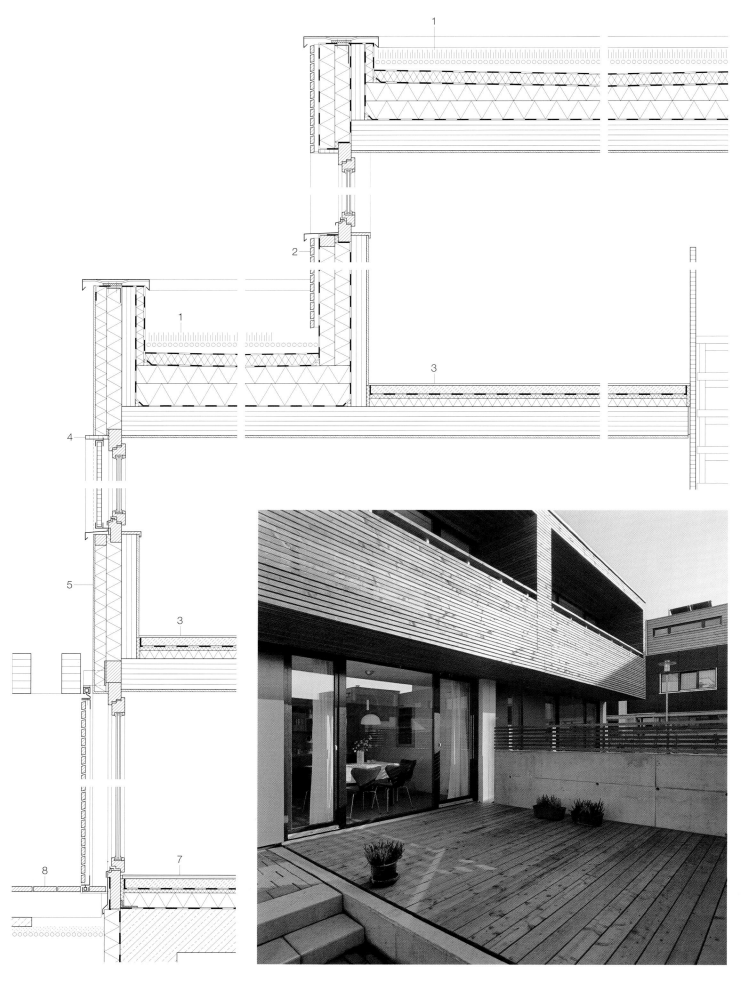

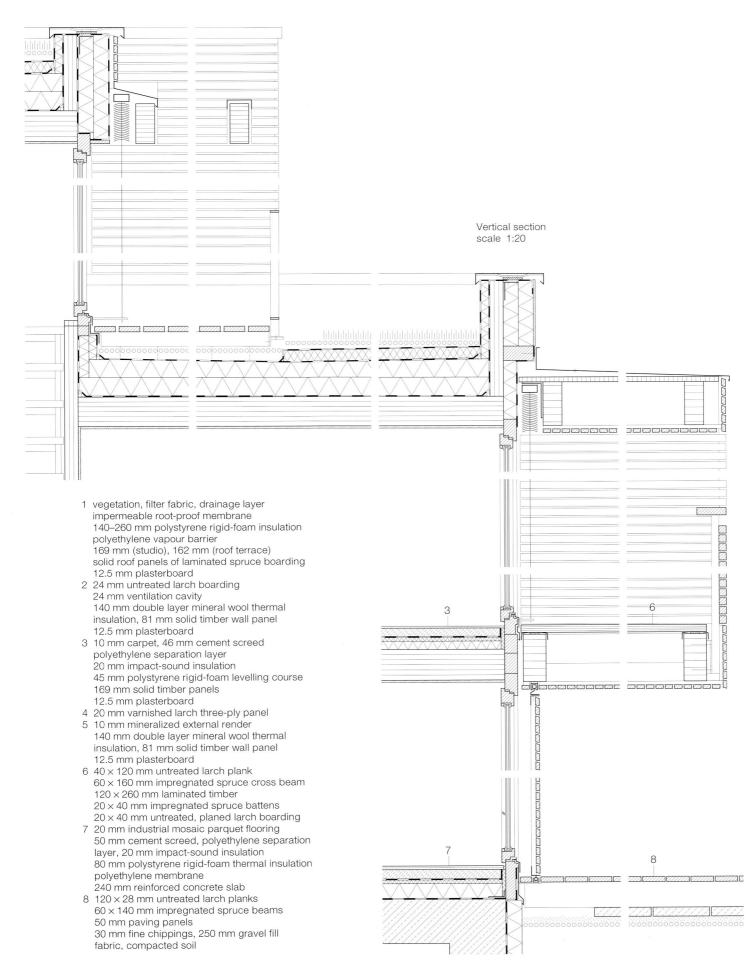

Vertical section
scale 1:20

1 vegetation, filter fabric, drainage layer
   impermeable root-proof membrane
   140–260 mm polystyrene rigid-foam insulation
   polyethylene vapour barrier
   169 mm (studio), 162 mm (roof terrace)
   solid roof panels of laminated spruce boarding
   12.5 mm plasterboard
2 24 mm untreated larch boarding
   24 mm ventilation cavity
   140 mm double layer mineral wool thermal
   insulation, 81 mm solid timber wall panel
   12.5 mm plasterboard
3 10 mm carpet, 46 mm cement screed
   polyethylene separation layer
   20 mm impact-sound insulation
   45 mm polystyrene rigid-foam levelling course
   169 mm solid timber panels
   12.5 mm plasterboard
4 20 mm varnished larch three-ply panel
5 10 mm mineralized external render
   140 mm double layer mineral wool thermal
   insulation, 81 mm solid timber wall panel
   12.5 mm plasterboard
6 40 × 120 mm untreated larch plank
   60 × 160 mm impregnated spruce cross beam
   120 × 260 mm laminated timber
   20 × 40 mm impregnated spruce battens
   20 × 40 mm untreated, planed larch boarding
7 20 mm industrial mosaic parquet flooring
   50 mm cement screed, polyethylene separation
   layer, 20 mm impact-sound insulation
   80 mm polystyrene rigid-foam thermal insulation
   polyethylene membrane
   240 mm reinforced concrete slab
8 120 × 28 mm untreated larch planks
   60 × 140 mm impregnated spruce beams
   50 mm paving panels
   30 mm fine chippings, 250 mm gravel fill
   fabric, compacted soil

Housing Development in Stuttgart

Architects: Kohlmayer Oberst Architects, Stuttgart

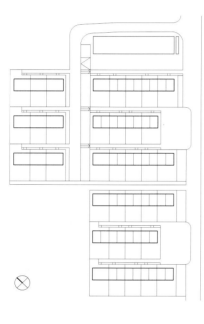

Project Details:
Usage: 37 terrace houses
24x 4-room (112 m²)
13x 5-room (134 m²)
Internal ceiling height: 2.4 m
Construction type: timber framework
Total floor area: 10,250 m²
Annual energy requirement for heating:
8.0–9.4 kWh/m²a
Construction cost: 8.45 million €
Construction time: 2002–2003

The residential area "Im Raiser", located on the site of former military barracks in Zuffenhausen, a northern suburb of Stuttgart, is a peaceful, garden suburb designed for young families. The architects were successful in an urban planning competition run in 1988 with their concept of a densely planned two- to three-storey development. The multi-stage competition was offered by the city council under the title of "cost, space and energy conservation" and was structured such that architects and construction companies collaborate in teams. The four most successful teams were subsequently invited to construct their projects on various sites; one of these teams consisted of the architects Kohlmayer Oberst with SWSG, a Stuttgart housing development construction company.

The section of the development allocated to this team comprises 37 terrace houses – arranged in modest rows of three to four units – which are interconnected by pedestrian routes. All houses are structured upon the same basic layout: the narrow service and communication core is located on the north-east side of the dwelling, with entry, staircase, kitchen and bathroom, while the living and bedrooms face the gardens to the south-west. The standard room size in the upper levels, approximately 16 m², allows flexibility of use – whether bedrooms, children's rooms, workrooms or studies – as the residents see fit. Two different house types have been achieved by varying the heights of the clear-cut cubic forms: a four-room house of 112 m² with roof terrace, and a five-room house of 134 m².

The internal organisation of the dwellings is clearly reflected in the facades; the fenestration in the north-eastern sides is restricted to small window elements while the south-western elevations offer room-high openings. These alternate in a chequerboard rhythm with the closed areas of the facades. Douglas fir sliding window shutters alleviate the formality of the otherwise rigid facade arrangement and effectively create interplay between the open and closed panels.

The decision to execute the terrace houses in a timber-frame construction system was a direct result of the original brief, which stipulated an economical housing project. Major advantages of this form of construction were the reduced construction time and the possibility of increasing living space through the minimisation of external wall dimensions. Wall and floor elements were predominantly prefabricated and assembled on site. Large-format three-ply Douglas fir panels were applied as cladding for the ventilated facades. The grey-coloured glazing of the panels supersedes the normal natural weathering of such timber elements.

Site plan
scale 1:2000

Sections · Floor plans
scale 1:250

A Basement
B Ground floor
C Upper level
D Roof level
   5-room house type
E Roof level
   roof-terrace house type

1 Store room
2 Kitchen
3 WC
4 Entrance
5 Living room
6 Bathroom
7 Room
8 Roof terrace

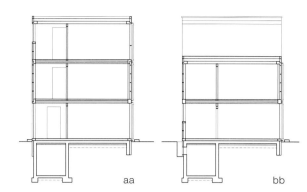

aa

bb

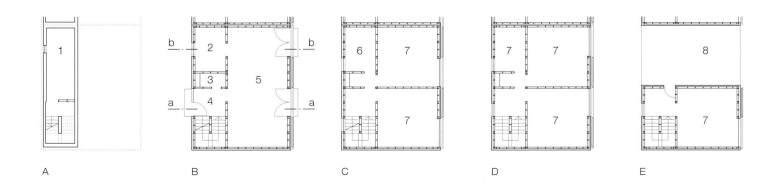

A

B

C

D

E

Vertical section · Horizontal section
scale 1:20

1 roof construction:
  extensive roof planting, EPDM membrane
  140 mm rigid-core polystyrene insulation
  mineral fibre insulation between
  100 × 180 mm solid timber rafters
  polyethylene vapour barrier
  20 mm counterbattens
  12.5 mm fibrous plasterboard
2 upper level floor construction:
  2 mm linoleum
  55 mm anhydrite floor screed
  polyethylene separation layer
  26 mm polyurethane insulation
  10 mm polystyrene levelling course
  22 mm oriented-strand board
  mineral fibre insulation between
  100 × 180 mm solid timber beams
  20 mm counterbattens
  12.5 mm fibrous plasterboard
3 external wall construction:
  22 mm three-ply Douglas fir panel
  20 mm counterbattens
  permeable facade membrane
  65 mm mineral wool thermal insulation
  15 mm oriented-strand board
  mineral wool insulation between
  60 x 120 mm solid timber framework element
  polyethylene vapour barrier
  12.5 mm fibrous plasterboard
4 double glazing: 4 mm float glass +
  16 mm cavity + 4 mm float glass
5 sliding window shutters:
  40 x 40 mm squared Douglas fir
6 precast concrete pavers in sand bed

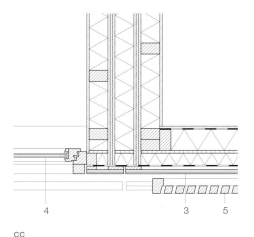

cc

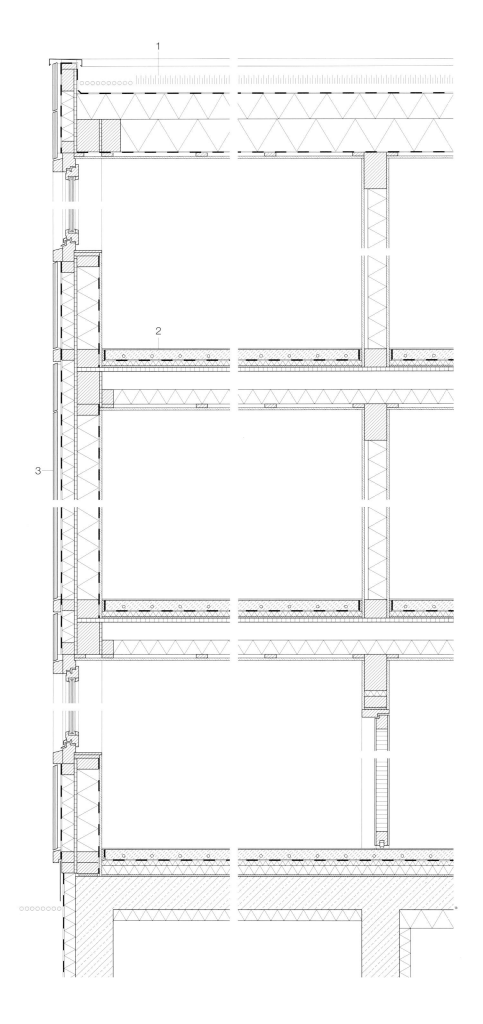

74

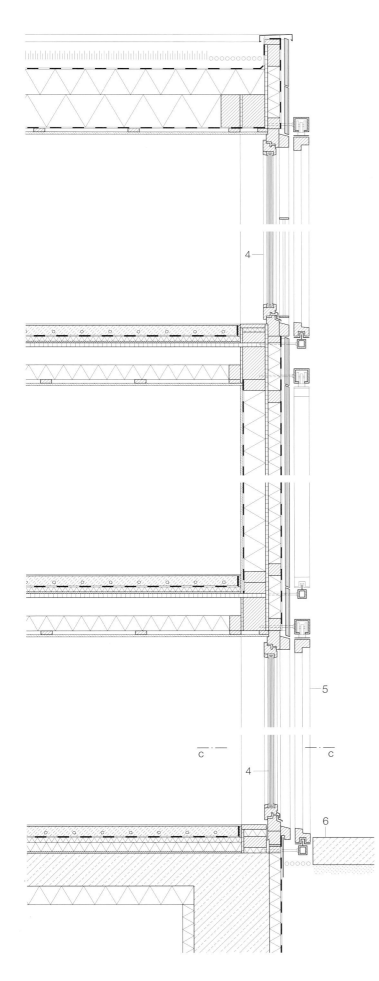

Holiday Houses in Hvide Sande

Architects: Cubo Arkitekter, Århus

Due to its unique location on the narrow headland between the North Sea and the Ringkobing Fjord, the former fishing village Hvide Sande has developed into one of the most popular holiday destinations in Denmark. 70 holiday houses have been constructed on the shore of Ringkobing Fjord.

Traditional local fishermen's cottages provided the inspiration for the black-painted rows of wooden dwellings which stretch out along the shoreline. The most noticeable feature of the development is the rhythm of the pitched roofs, determining the fundamental grid upon which the two different house types are based. Directly fronting the water's edge are the single-storey houses; they are divided into two equal halves and are accommodated beneath two of the pitched roofs. One side of each house contains the generous living area with integrated kitchen, while two bedrooms and two bathrooms can be found in the other side. The dwellings in the rear row are of two-storey construction, thereby ensuring the residents the desired views of Ringkobing Fjord. These houses are set beneath a single roof and provide only one bedroom each, located on the ground floor. The living spaces on the upper levels include north-facing loggias and south-facing balconies.

Both house types include ancillary entrance structures which, in conjunction with the main buildings, create private inner courtyards. These are separated from the neighbouring court-yards by high wall elements. The holiday houses make the most of views of the water by opening out to the south, with large windows set in the gable walls, and abundant outdoor seating areas.

Project details:
Usage: 70 holiday houses
Internal ceiling height: type A 3.0 m
                                       type B 2.4/3.0 m
Construction type: reinforced concrete
Total floor area: 7,900 m²
Total site area: 31,000 m²
Construction time: 1st building stage 2004
                                       2nd building stage 2005
                                       3rd building stage 6/2006

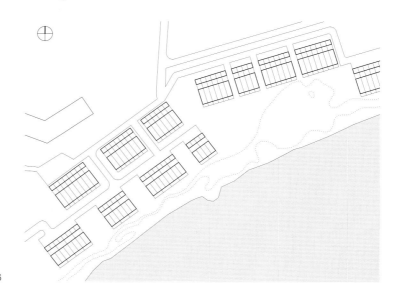

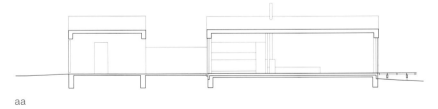

aa

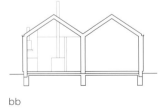

bb

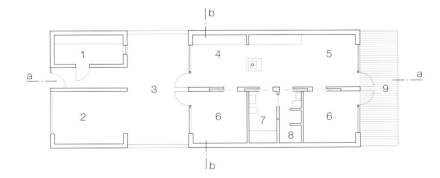

1 Utility room
2 Carport
3 Courtyard
4 Kitchen
5 Living room
6 Bedroom
7 Bathroom
8 Sauna
9 Terrace

Terrace house type A

Sections · Floor plan
scale 1:250
Vertical section
scale 1:20

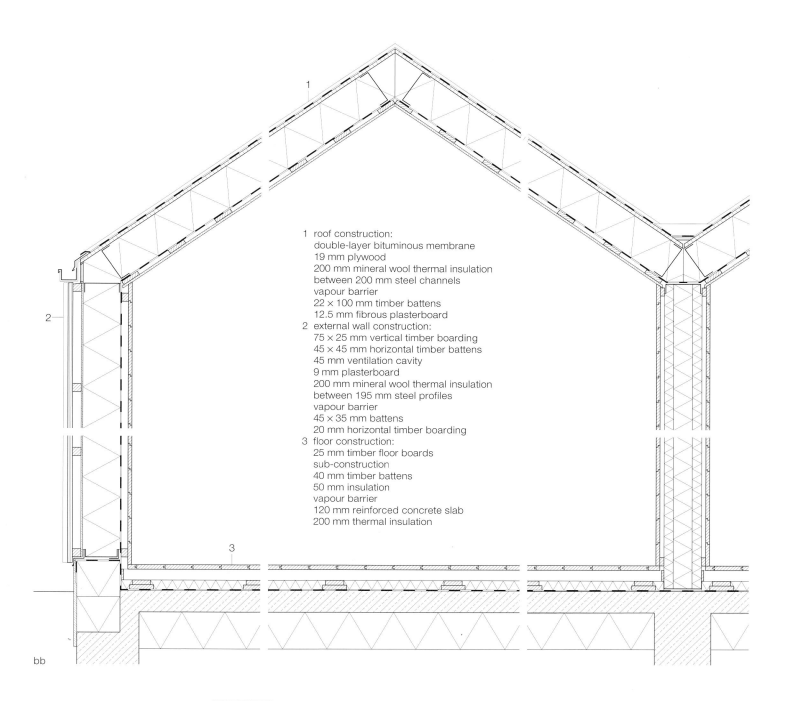

1 roof construction:
   double-layer bituminous membrane
   19 mm plywood
   200 mm mineral wool thermal insulation
   between 200 mm steel channels
   vapour barrier
   22 × 100 mm timber battens
   12.5 mm fibrous plasterboard
2 external wall construction:
   75 × 25 mm vertical timber boarding
   45 × 45 mm horizontal timber battens
   45 mm ventilation cavity
   9 mm plasterboard
   200 mm mineral wool thermal insulation
   between 195 mm steel profiles
   vapour barrier
   45 × 35 mm battens
   20 mm horizontal timber boarding
3 floor construction:
   25 mm timber floor boards
   sub-construction
   40 mm timber battens
   50 mm insulation
   vapour barrier
   120 mm reinforced concrete slab
   200 mm thermal insulation

bb

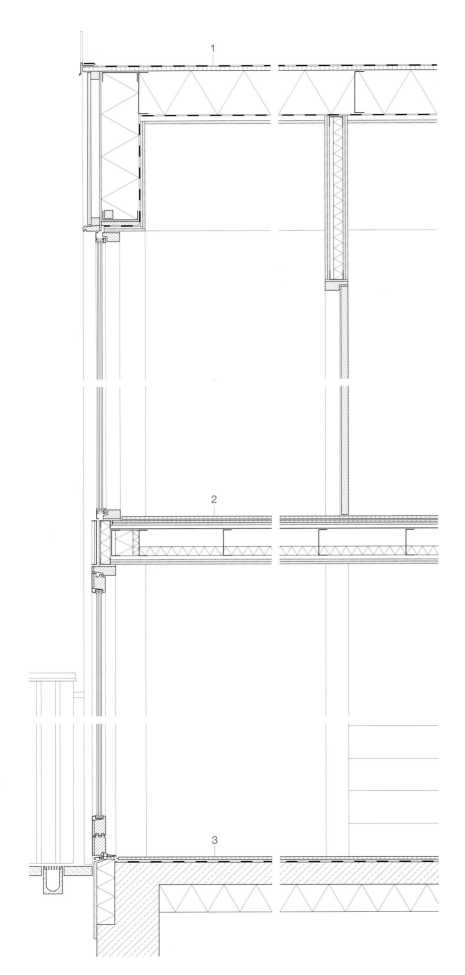

1 roof construction:
  double-layer bituminous membrane
  19 mm plywood
  200 mm mineral wool thermal insulation
  between 200 mm steel channels
  vapour barrier
  22 × 100 mm timber battens
  12.5 mm fibrous plasterboard
2 floor construction:
  14 mm laminate flooring
  felt impact-sound insulation
  12 mm plywood
  13 mm plasterboard
  20 mm trapezoidal sheet metal
  50 mm insulation between
  150 mm steel channels
  22 mm timber battens
  2 × 13 mm fibrous plasterboard
3 ground floor construction:
  14 mm laminate flooring
  felt impact-sound insulation
  vapour barrier
  120 mm reinforced concrete slab
  150 mm thermal insulation

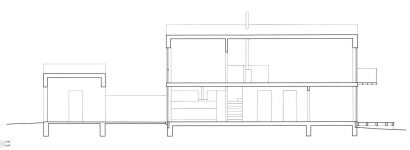

Terrace house type B

Section · Floor plans
scale 1:250
Vertical section
scale 1:20

A Ground floor
B First floor

1 Utility room
2 Courtyard
3 Kitchen
4 Sauna
5 Bathroom
6 Bedroom
7 Terrace
8 Living room
9 Balcony

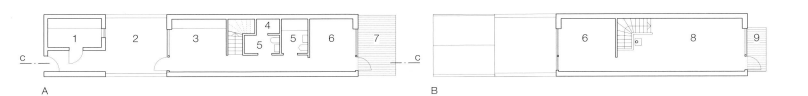

A

B

Terraced Housing in Mulhouse

Architects: Anne Lacaton & Jean Philippe Vassal, Paris

Project details:
Usage: 14 terrace houses
Floor area: 2x 5-room type 175 m²
                               6x 4-room type 175 m²
                               4x 3-room type 128 m²
                               2x 2-room type 102 m²
Internal ceiling height: 3.0 m (ground floor)
                               2.4 m (first floor)
                               4.3 m (greenhouse)
Construction type: steel/reinforced concrete
Total floor area: 2,243 m²
Total site area: 1,690 m²
Construction cost: 1.05 million €
Date of completion: January 2005

Sections · Floor plans
scale 1:400   1 Living
                               2 Garage
A First floor   3 Bedroom
B Ground floor   4 Greenhouse

To commemorate its 150th anniversary the housing department of Mulhouse, in Alsace, invited five teams of architects – Shigeru Ban & De Gastines, Lacaton & Vassal, Lewis & Block, Poitevin & Raynaud and Jean Nouvel – to plan a social housing project of 60 modern apartments.

The housing department began constructing estates for factory workers in 1853. East of the first historical location, a site which had originally accommodated a textile factory was selected for the new housing project. The site was subdivided into four parallel east-west lots, measuring approximately 27 by 60 metres, and a fifth triangular lot running perpendicular. The teams were required to develop two-storey terraced dwellings of various sizes. Lacaton & Vassal pursued their concept of "spacious apartments on small budgets" which they had successfully employed on many smaller projects; their fourteen residential units, ranging from 102 to 175 m², are twice as large as standard French social housing for the same cost.

With the exception of four dwellings, which are rotated on plan at the eastern end of the site, the terrace houses stretch the width of the twenty-metre site. By offsetting the often oblique internal walls, each dwelling is provided with different amounts of space on the ground and first floors. The ground floor is primarily given over to a large multi-purpose room, incorporating living, dining and cooking functions, with only the integrated garage and a modest sanitary cell completing the layout. The first floor of the larger houses contains a number of bedrooms, while in the smaller dwellings the first floor is only subdivided by the sanitary cell. Every house benefits from an individual greenhouse varying in size from 19 to almost 50 m².

The three-metre-high ground floor is constructed of precast concrete elements; prefabricated slabs are supported by longitudinal beams, supported by rows of columns. This pedestal acts as the foundation for three rows of standard greenhouses. Clad in corrugated translucent and opaque polycarbonate panels, the galvanized steel structure creates 4.5-metre-high spaces. The southern-most row is uninsulated, whereas the other two rows have insulated ceilings suspended from the load-bearing structure. The external walls are constructed of translucent, corrugated panels and full-height windows with opaque sliding shutters; the lightweight internal party walls function independently of the external load-bearing system. Aluminium-backed curtains aid thermal insulation. A true loft character has been achieved. Open plan layouts, untreated concrete surfaces, simple galvanized spiral stairs and synthetic wall panels all combine to create the atmosphere of a renovated factory building.

aa

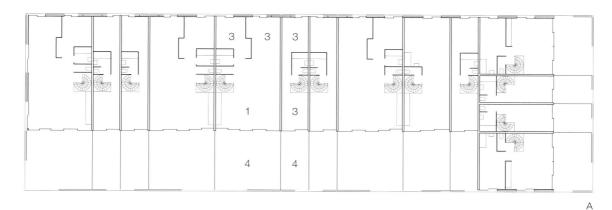

A

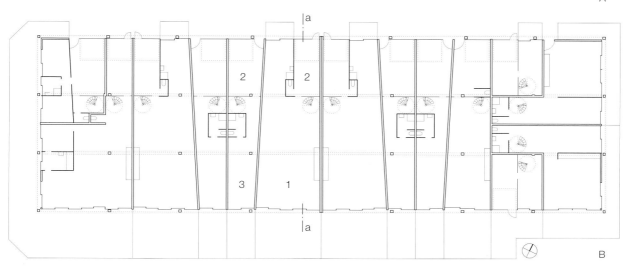

B

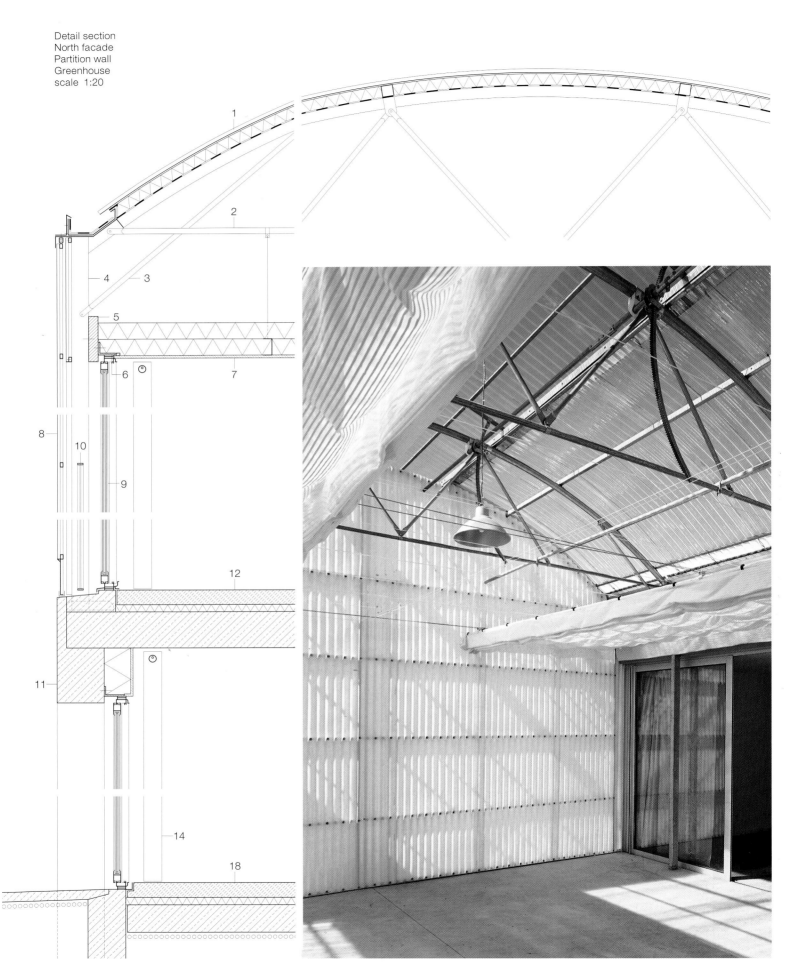

Detail section
North facade
Partition wall
Greenhouse
scale 1:20

1

2

4   3

5

6   7

8

10

9

12

11

14

18

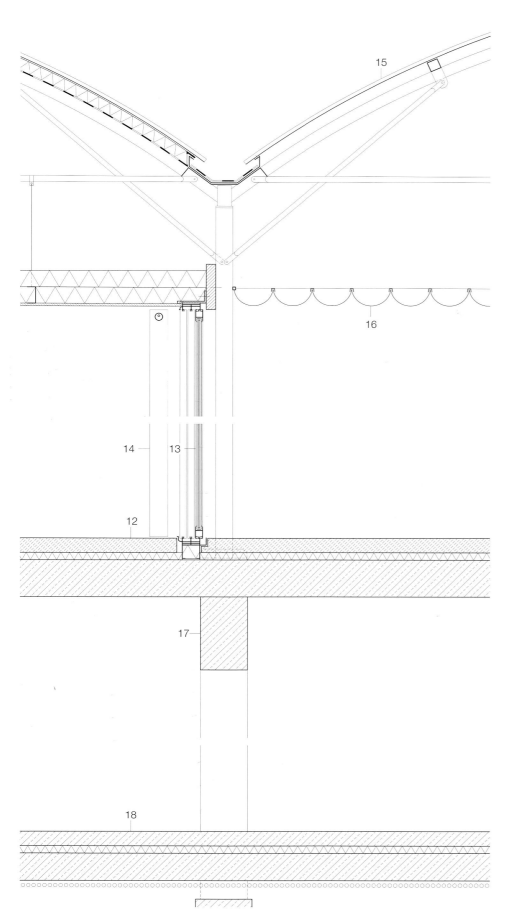

1 roof construction:
   20 mm opaque corr. polycarbonate panel
   60 mm glass wool thermal insulation between
   60 × 60 mm SHS steel purlins
   vapour barrier
   60 × 60 mm SHS steel arched beam
2 Ø 37 mm steel tension rod
3 Ø 27 mm steel diagonal rod
4 90 × 50 mm RHS steel column
5 250 × 50 mm timber lintel
6 70 × 90 mm steel angle
7 suspended ceiling construction:
   180 mm rock wool thermal insulation
   sub-construction
   15 mm plasterboard
8 sliding shutters:
   aluminium frame
   20 mm corrugated polycarbonate panels
9 double sliding door:
   aluminium frame, extruded profile
   double glazing (4 mm toughened glass +
   16 mm cavity + 4 mm toughened glass)
10 10 × 50 mm steel flat balustrade
11 585 × 250 mm precast reinforced concrete
   edge beam
12 first floor construction:
   80 mm screed, waxed
   40 mm insulation
   200 mm reinforced concrete
13 triple sliding door:
   aluminium frame, extruded profile
   triple glazing (4 mm glass + 10 mm cavity
   + 4 mm toughened glass)
14 double-layer insulating curtain:
   reflective aluminium textile (external)
   wool fabric (internal)
15 roof construction, greenhouse:
   20 mm translucent corr. polycarbonate panel
   60 × 60 mm SHS steel purlins
   60 × 60 mm SHS steel arched beam
16 manually adjustable sun-shading awning
17 400 × 250 mm precast reinforced concrete
   beam
18 ground floor construction:
   80 mm screed, waxed
   40 mm insulation
   150 mm reinforced concrete slab
   base course

Housing Groups in Almere

Architects: UN Studio Van Berkel & Bos, Amsterdam

Project details:
Usage: 48 dwelling units
                            in three house types
Floor areas: 12x type a 150 m²
                            10x type b 165 m²
                            26x type c 180 m²
Construction type: reinforced concrete
                            and steel modules
Internal ceiling height: 2.62 m/2.43 m
Total floor area: 9,640 m²
Total site area: 15,147 m²
Date of completion: 2001

Site plan   scale 1:5000

Simultaneous desires for maximum flexibility and individuality of expression were the driving forces behind this housing project designed by the UN Studio, Amsterdam. The housing scheme was realized as part of the building exhibition, Expo 2001, and located on the Northeast Polder in Almere, a planned township founded in 1976.

In order to unite flexibility and individuality, the architects developed a modular system. Forty-eight dwelling units were constructed to meet the clients' requirements; in addition to a row of detached houses, the scheme includes terraced houses in groups varying from two to six units. The individual built forms are combined in such a way as to ensure views of the water. Generous spacing between the units guarantees ample privacy and sufficient natural daylight. Surrounded by water the projecting terraces resemble the decks of a ship, and offer the residents additional private outdoor spaces.

The modular system is applied not only to the scheme as a whole, but also to the individual housing units. The basic module is formed by stacking two concrete elements, each 6 × 10 metres on plan and three metres high. By offsetting the units to each other, a 2.5-metre-wide terrace is formed, and the addition of a third storey allows an additional roof terrace to be created. In the case of the detached houses, the sculptural effect is further heightened by turning the storey units at right angles to each other. The location of the kitchen, bathroom and stairs were left open as long as possible to accommodate different lifestyles.

In order to enlarge the residential volume to meet client demands, additional prefabricated steel-frame box elements, 2.5 × 6 metres on plan, can be added at various points.

The concrete blocks are double-clad with rectangular slate panels; the sculptural character of the scheme as a whole is further enhanced by the cladding continuing on the underside of the blocks.

In contrast with the basic structure, the extension elements are clad in chestnut-coloured plywood panels.

Cantilevering over the water by up to 5 metres, the houses generate ample reflections, further intensifying the visual impression of interacting solid blocks and open voids.

A Detached house:
  Floor plans · Sections
B Terraced house, 2 Dwelling units:
  Floor plans
C Terraced house, 3 Dwelling units:
  Floor plans
scale 1:400

1 Living room with kitchen
2 Room
3 Terrace

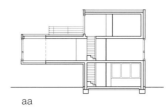

aa

bb

A

B

C

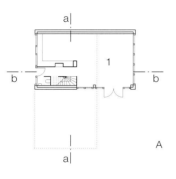

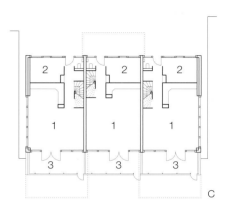

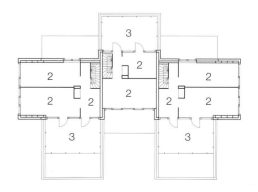

D Terraced house,
 3 Dwelling units:
 Floor plans
E Terraced house,
 5 Dwelling units:
 Floor plans
F Terraced house,
 4 Dwelling units:
 Floor plans
G Terraced house,
 6 Dwelling units:
 Floor plans
scale 1:400

1 Living room with kitchen
2 Room
3 Terrace

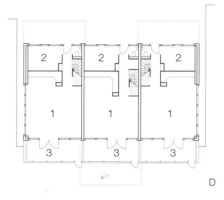

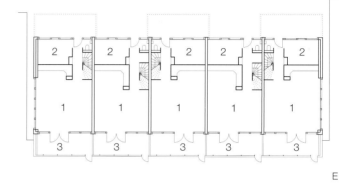

D

E

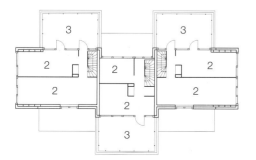

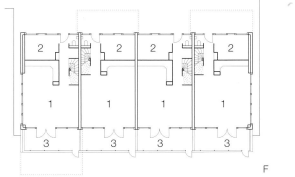

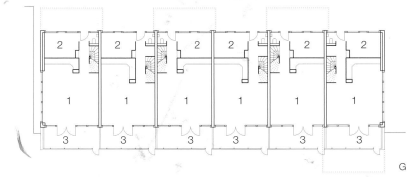

F

G

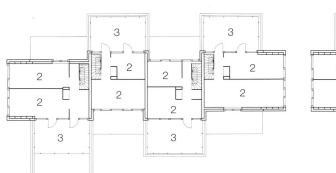

Terraced Housing in Kanoya

Architects: NKS architects, Fukuoka

Located on the pastoral, southern Japanese island of Kyushu, this development is a compact blend of residential and commercial units. Two large commercial units are accommodated within the anthracite-coloured ground floor while nine small dwellings comprise the two upper levels. The access to the terrace houses is from the southern side, with each dwelling having a parking bay, which is offset on plan and reached via a private stair. The image of the building is greatly influenced by the rhythm of the concrete stairways and the car parking. Different types of terraced dwellings reach through the depth of the building and are closely interlocked with each other. This interlocking on the second floor enabled the architects to create three discrete unit types, varying both in size and floor layout, in spite of the compartmentalized nature of the construction. The smallest apartment comprises a living space, kitchen and bathroom on the first floor with a minute sleeping space above being reached by a ladder. In the other two layouts, the bathroom is located on the second floor, with access via a lightweight steel stair. One dwelling type includes a deep, south-facing outdoor seating area. All internal walls are constructed of exposed concrete and the floors are of parquet. In spite of the limited floor area available, the overall impression of the dwellings is one of space and light; each dwelling is arranged around a two-storey void and lit by extensive glazing in the southern facade.

Due to Japan's sub-tropical climate, the majority of the energy required goes towards cooling. Each dwelling has been provided with an air-conditioner by the property-owner. Louvered windows were installed in both the north and south facades, allowing cross-ventilation to occur and thereby reducing energy consumption. Further protection from the summer heat is provided by deep eaves to the south and thermal insulation within the flat-roof construction.

Project details:
Building type: terraced housing
Usage: 9x residential units
                     2x commercial units
Floor area: 3x type a 43.65 m²
                     3x type b 26.00 m²
                     3x type c 45.50 m²
Construction type: reinforced concrete
Total floor area: 505.96 m²
Total internal volume: 1,395.96 m³
Total site area: 2244.36 m²
Construction cost: 1,189 €/m²
Date of completion: April 2002

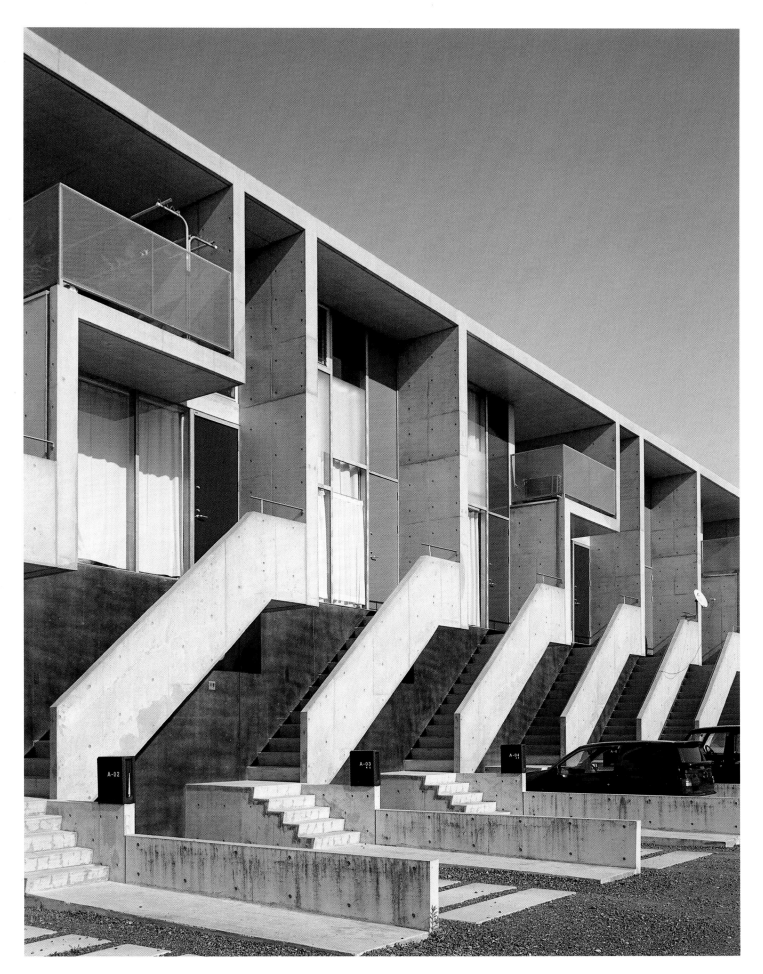

Isometric

Floor plans · Sections
scale 1:400

A Second floor
B First floor
C Ground floor

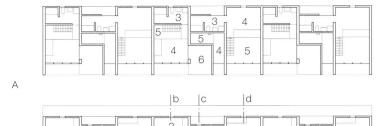

A

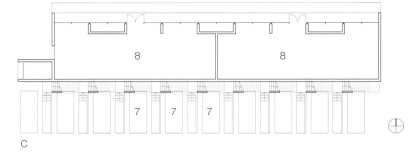

B

C

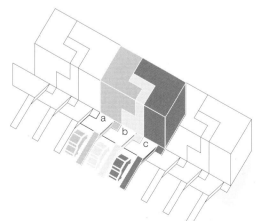

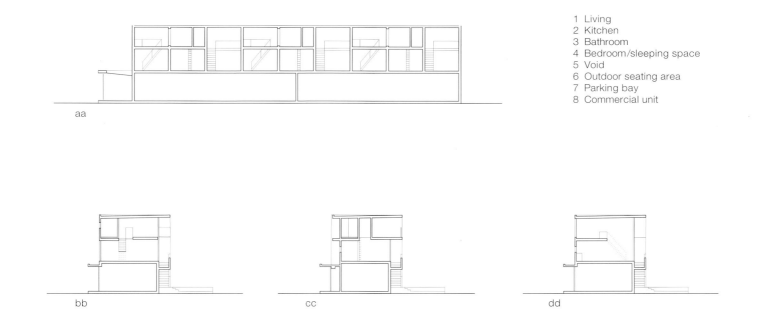

aa

bb   cc   dd

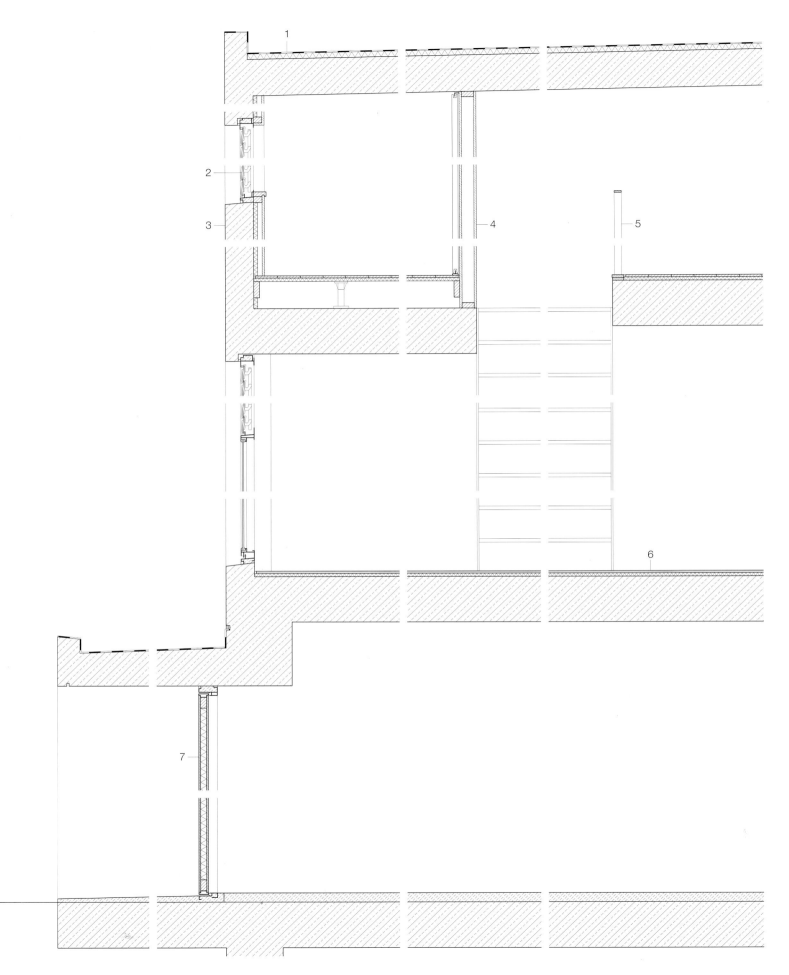

Vertical section
Horizontal section
scale 1:20

1 roof construction:
   impermeable membrane
   30 mm polystyrene thermal
   insulation
   200 mm reinforced concrete slab
2 aluminium profile louvred window
   with 5 mm toughened glass
3 external wall construction:
   150 mm exposed concrete
   20 mm polystyrene thermal
   insulation
   45 mm sub-construction
   12.5 mm plasterboard
4 internal wall construction:
   12.5 mm plasterboard
   65 mm sub-construction

   12.5 mm impermeable
   plasterboard
5 38 × 9 mm steel profile
   balustrade
6 floor construction:
   12 mm timber parquet
   18 mm impact-sound insulation
   250 mm reinforced concrete slab
7 steel gate
8 5 mm toughened glass,
   fixed in steel profile
9 aluminium casement window with
   5 mm toughened glass
   in aluminium profile
10 30 mm screed
11 external stair: 30 mm screed
   150 mm reinforced concrete
12 100 × 50 × 4.5 mm steel profile
13 50 mm pine door
14 8 mm cement fibreboard

ee

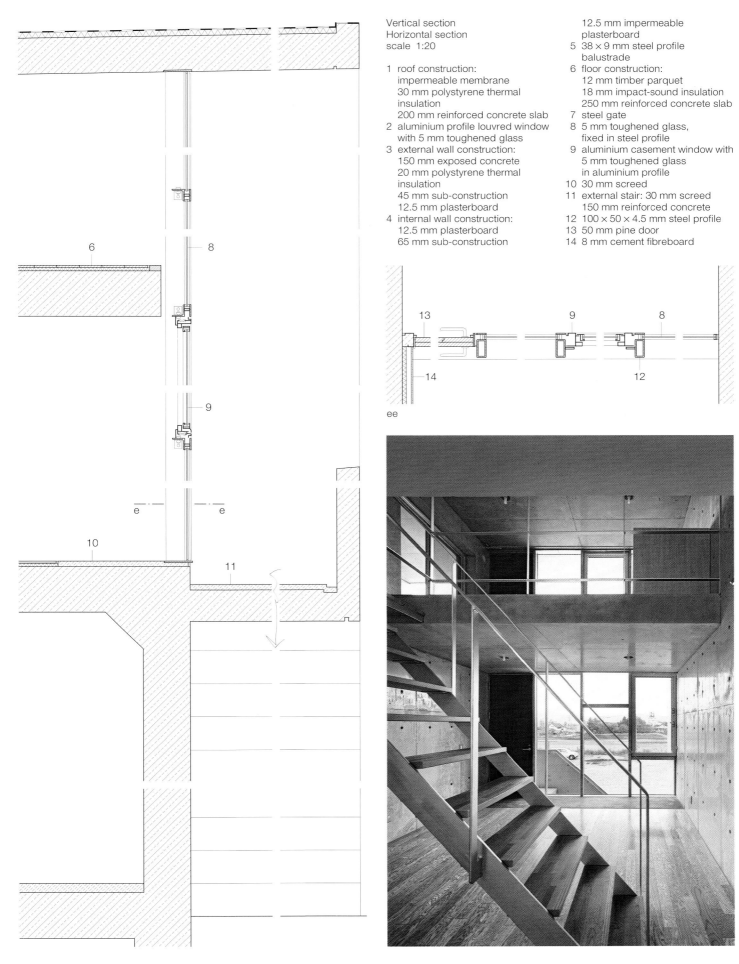

Sound-Barrier Terraced Housing in Hilversum

Architect: Maurice Nio, Rotterdam

Site plan
scale 1:2500

Twelve terrace houses are integrated into a sound-barrier wall running parallel to the main road between Diependaal and Hilversum. Crouching down in the acoustic shadow of the barrier wall, these houses successfully forge the transition between the roadway and the neighbouring residential estate. By creating a housing scheme as low-scale as possible, the architects managed to keep noise down while still creating well-illuminated dwellings. From the road, which runs along the top of the causeway, the houses are scarcely visible. Behind the translucent noise barrier one is barely aware of the flat silver-grey roofs.

The cantilevered boxes are known as "the Cyclopses" because they appear to be observing the onlooker. The living space on the first floor cantilevers well out, natural illumination being predominantly available from one direction, causing the 90 m² lower level to be distinctly smaller than the upper level. Sheltered beneath the cantilevered living room, the centrally positioned entrance is approached through a vestibule. Additional daylight reaches this fully internal zone through bull's-eye skylights in the ceiling. Two naturally lit rooms, as well as a windowless bathroom and store, are connected by a small corridor. The other side of the ground floor is taken up by the fully integrated garage. A double-flight stair connects to the first floor which measures 120 m². Accommodated within this level are the large, funnel-shaped living space, the kitchen, an additional bedroom and bathroom. The repetition of the angular units made two-directional illumination of the living spaces possible. Sheltered roof terraces for the residents were also created.

The load-bearing system is of prefabricated concrete, the in-situ concrete in the lower area clad in clinker brickwork, while the underside of the first floor is finished with silver-coloured composite resin panels.

In spite of the location and initial scepticism, the futuristic appearance of the scheme ensured plenty of interested buyers.

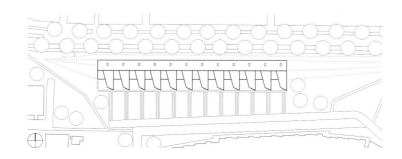

Section
Floor plans
scale 1:250

A First floor
B Ground floor

1 Entrance
2 Bedroom
3 Bathroom
4 Store
5 Garage
6 Kitchen
7 Living
8 Cupboard
9 Terrace

Project details:
Usage: 12 terrace houses
Floor area: 12x 120 m² (4-room)
Internal ceiling height: 2.26 – 3.20 m
Construction type: reinforced concrete
Total floor area: 2,484 m²
Total site area: 5,911 m²
Construction cost: 3.29 million €
Construction time: 2001

aa

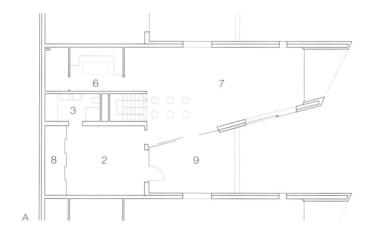

A

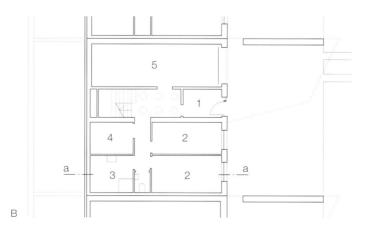

B

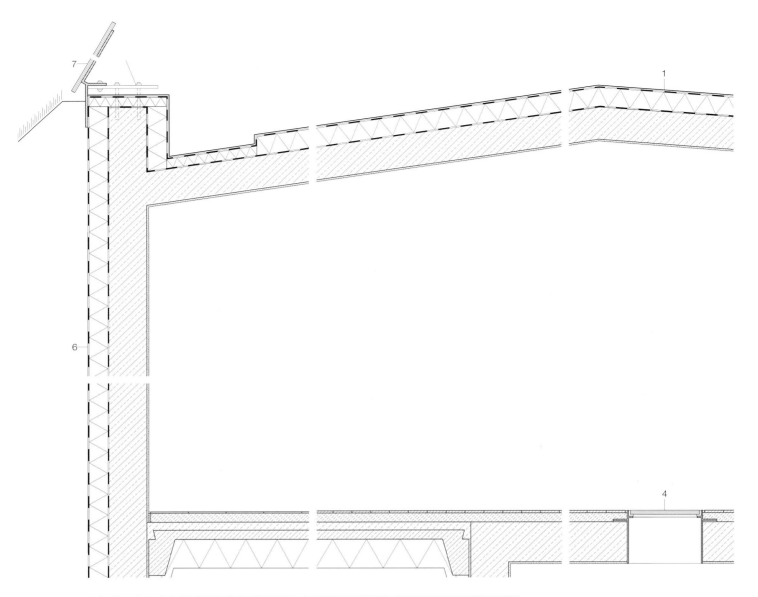

Section   scale 1:20
1 roof construction:
   1.2 mm PVC roof membrane, silver
   coloured, vapour barrier
   100 mm rigid-foam thermal insulation
   vapour barrier
   180 mm reinforced concrete
   3 mm sprayed plaster
2 Meranti window frame, double glazing
3 cantilevered floor construction:
   1.2 mm PVC roof membrane, silver
   coloured, vapour barrier
   60 mm rigid-foam thermal insulation
   vapour barrier, screed, with gradient
   220 mm r. c. slab, vapour barrier
   thermal insulation between
   45 × 60 mm timber rafters
   vapour barrier
   ventilation cavity, aluminium profile
   10 mm composite resin panel
4 bull's-eye: 5 mm steel frame
   23 mm lam. safety glass
5 aluminium garage door, coated
6 sub-terranean wall construction:
   bituminous membrane
   100 mm thermal insulation
   impermeable membrane
   200 mm reinforced concrete
   3 mm sprayed plaster
7 sound insulating glazing
   17 mm polycarbonate green

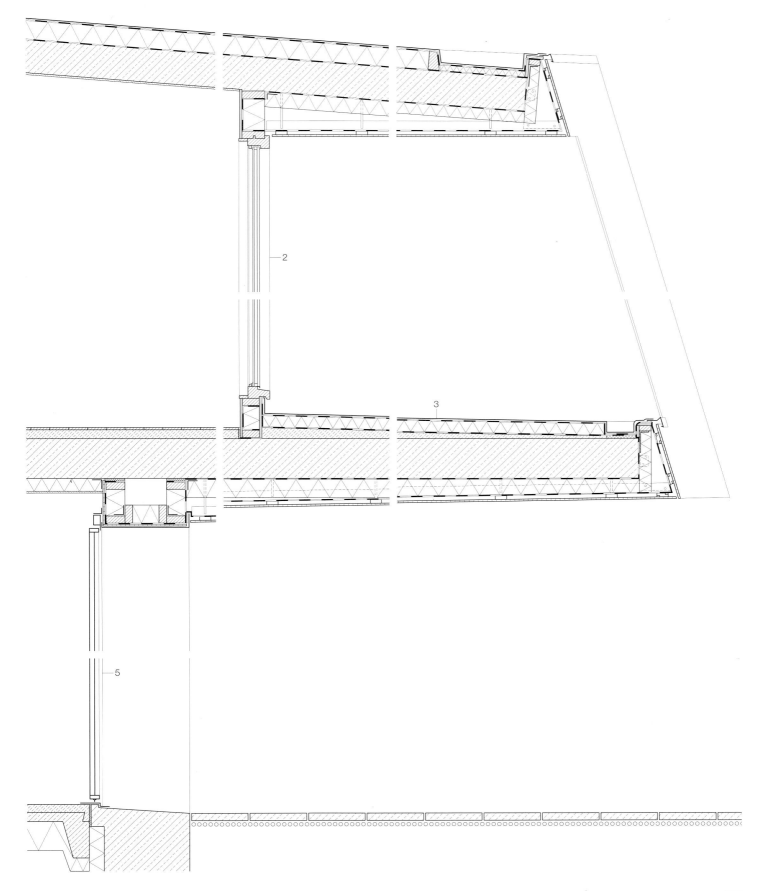

Terraced Housing Row in Munich

Architects: von Seidlein, Fischer, Konrad, Röhrl, Munich

This row of terraced houses can be found south of Munich, on a block of land immediately adjacent to the river Isar. The original site development was extensively damaged during the Second World War and was, of necessity, demolished; only the small pilgrimage church of St Anna, adjoining the allotment, survived. The new, two-storey housing development keeps a respectful distance from the chapel; the space in between plays host to a mature stock of trees and serves as a communal zone for the residents. The ten terraced houses open onto this green space with room-high windows. The elevations to the street are similarly extensively glazed; privacy is ensured, however, by the individual walled forecourts which simultaneously protect each dwelling and provide semi-open entrances.

The fundamental planning concept consists of long, narrow units of 6.5 by 17.4 metres, with the principal rooms being located behind the facades and ancillary rooms situated in the centre. Skylights illuminate these internal rooms while the open, single-flight staircase ensures that light also penetrates down to the ground-floor corridor. Varying only in their depth, the first-storey rooms are approximately three metres wide; by removing a partition wall two rooms can be combined to create a larger one.

While the development contains a complete basement level, only a part of it is given over to the private dwellings; the communal underground car park provides two parking spaces per dwelling and additional storage space for bicycles. Each house has a stair within the basement storey ensuring individual and private access to the dwellings.

Every principal room has access to a balcony or terrace facing either the communal green space to the north-west or the private courtyards to the south-east. This variety offers the residents the alternative of selecting sunny or shady spots at various times of the day or year. Sun-shading is provided by the application of folding aluminium shutters to the external corners of the outdoor living areas, and permanent concrete dividers protect the privacy of the residents. The issue of acoustic insulation has been dealt with by the architects in as much detail as that of privacy; a five-centimetre-wide separation joint divides the two layers of the in-situ concrete party walls. The separation joint commences at the upper level of the bottom slab which functions as the foundation for the entire development. Although the development consists of ten terraced houses, the care and attention given to the planning has ensured a quality of design comparable to that of single-family houses; the residents' privacy is respected and the individual units, at 197 m², are spacious and open.

Site plan   scale 1:2500

Project details:
Usage: 10 terraced houses
Floor area per house: 197 m²
Internal ceiling height: 2.49 m
Construction type: reinforced concrete
Total site area: 6,745 m²
Construction cost: 4 million €
Date of completion: 2001

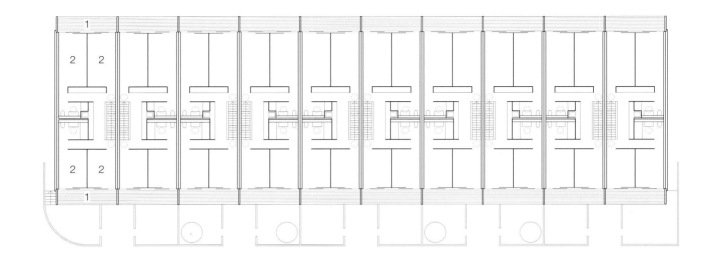

A

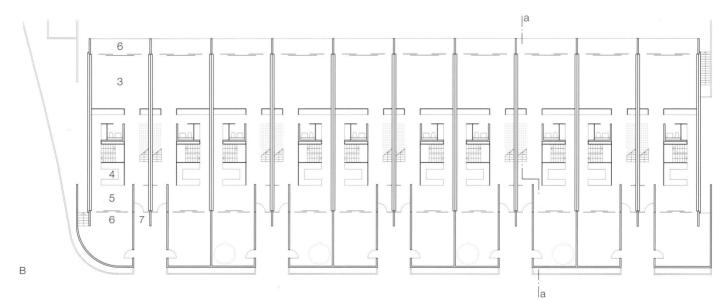

B

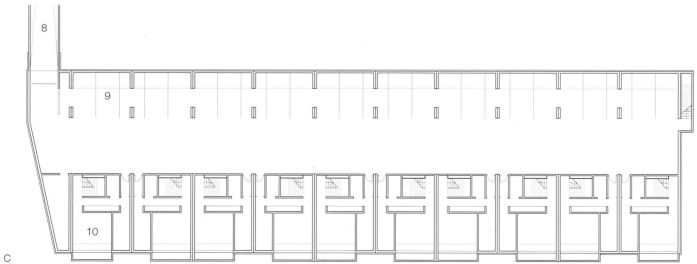

C

Floor plans · section
scale 1:400

A First floor
B Ground floor
C Basement

1 Balcony
2 Bedroom
3 Living
4 Kitchen
5 Dining
6 Terrace
7 Entrance
8 Car park driveway
9 Parking space
10 Private basement

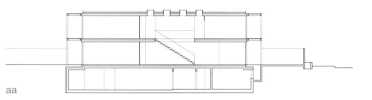

aa

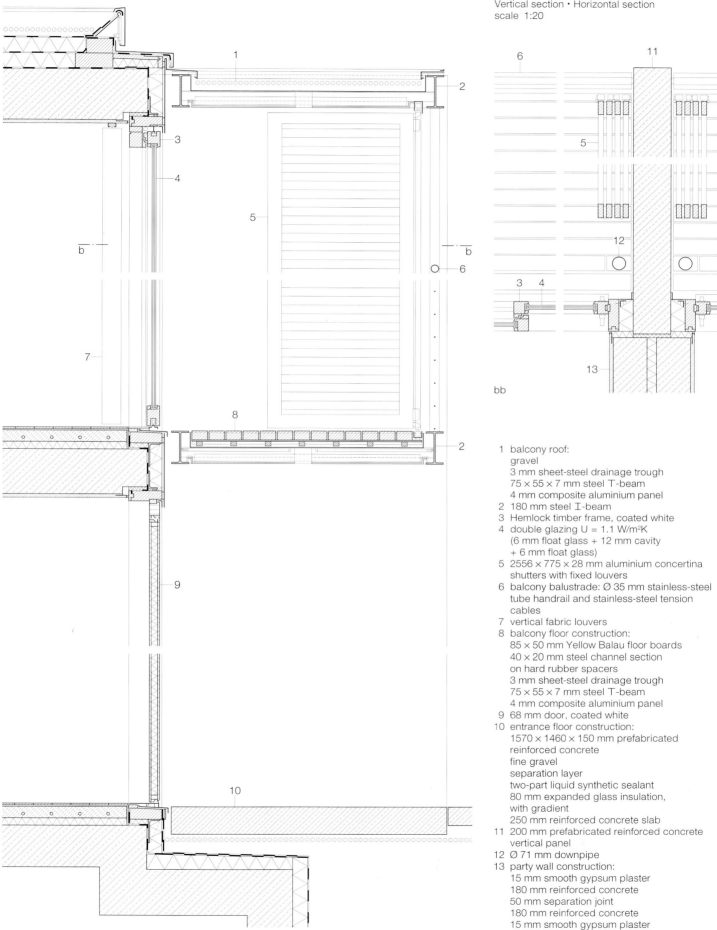

bb

1 balcony roof:
   gravel
   3 mm sheet-steel drainage trough
   75 × 55 × 7 mm steel T-beam
   4 mm composite aluminium panel
2 180 mm steel I-beam
3 Hemlock timber frame, coated white
4 double glazing U = 1.1 W/m²K
   (6 mm float glass + 12 mm cavity
   + 6 mm float glass)
5 2556 × 775 × 28 mm aluminium concertina
   shutters with fixed louvers
6 balcony balustrade: Ø 35 mm stainless-steel
   tube handrail and stainless-steel tension
   cables
7 vertical fabric louvers
8 balcony floor construction:
   85 × 50 mm Yellow Balau floor boards
   40 × 20 mm steel channel section
   on hard rubber spacers
   3 mm sheet-steel drainage trough
   75 × 55 × 7 mm steel T-beam
   4 mm composite aluminium panel
9 68 mm door, coated white
10 entrance floor construction:
   1570 × 1460 × 150 mm prefabricated
   reinforced concrete
   fine gravel
   separation layer
   two-part liquid synthetic sealant
   80 mm expanded glass insulation,
   with gradient
   250 mm reinforced concrete slab
11 200 mm prefabricated reinforced concrete
   vertical panel
12 Ø 71 mm downpipe
13 party wall construction:
   15 mm smooth gypsum plaster
   180 mm reinforced concrete
   50 mm separation joint
   180 mm reinforced concrete
   15 mm smooth gypsum plaster

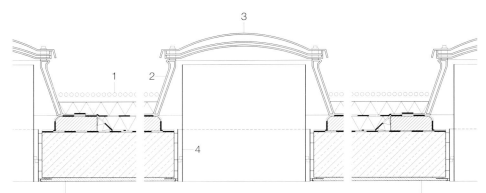

Vertical section   scale 1:20

1 roof construction:
   50 mm gravel
   80 mm XPS insulation (extruded polystyrene)
   impermeable PE-C membrane
   (chlorinated polyethylene)
   80 mm EPS insulation (expanded polystyrene)
   4 mm bituminous membrane
   250 mm reinforced concrete slab
   15 mm smooth gypsum plaster
2 Ø 900 mm glass-fibre reinforced plastic ring
3 skylight:
   external shell, polycarbonate
   internal shell, glass acrylic
4 3 mm powder-coated steel skylight surround
5 stair balustrade:
   35 × 25 mm oak handrail, oiled
   25 × 25 mm steel posts
   25 × 10 mm flat steel plates
   Ø 10 mm steel rods
6 237 × 10 mm flat steel plates
7 250 × 10 mm flat steel stringboard
8 270 × 50 mm oak stair goings,
   waxed and oiled
   on 250 × 10 mm flat steel plates
9 floor construction:
   12 mm oak multi-layer strip parquet flooring,
   waxed and oiled
   70 mm cement screed for underfloor heating
   20 mm EPS impact-sound insulation
   20 mm EPS base course
   250 mm reinforced concrete slab

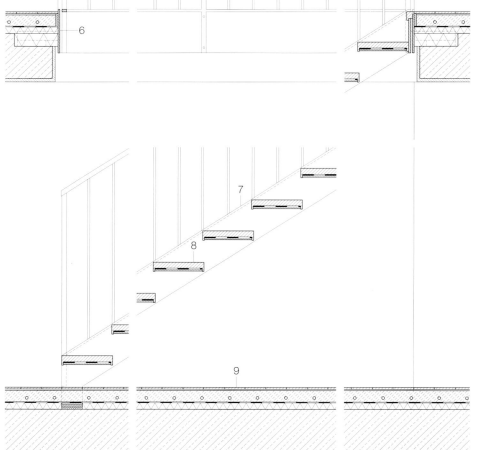

Semi-Detached Houses in Münchenstein

Architects: Steinmann & Schmid, Basle

These semi-detached houses are situated in a small township not far from Basle – with a classical pitched roof the structure is unobtrusive yet self-assured. The initial impression is that of a single-family dwelling: the narrow gable elevation effectively conceals the comparatively long side elevations from the street. Not until the dwellings are approached from the front, along the side path, does it become clear that there are two discrete entrances. The two separate residences only share a services room in the basement and the air-raid shelter, a prerequisite in Switzerland. In contrast to the majority of semi-detached houses, the floor plans here are neither identical nor symmetrical. Not even the common party-wall runs in a straight line through the building; it is set off on the ground floor.

The residents of the front house have a larger living space on the ground floor and the roof terrace above the double garage, while those in the rear house preside over more space in the upper levels and garden terrace area. The principle planning concept is consistent, however: the four-metre-deep living- and bedrooms are oriented to the south, overlooking the garden, whereas bathrooms and other ancillary rooms are stretched out behind the north facade. The uppermost level of both dwellings is partially given over to roomy, well-lit gallery spaces which are only separated from the single-flight stairs by the balustrade.

The elevational treatment is a direct result of the layout, having been determined by internal usage and external orientation. Narrow aluminium-framed windows are provided for the ancillary rooms to the north while the living and sleeping spaces are illuminated by way of larger timber-framed windows. These timber-framed windows are of various sizes and articulate the brown rendered facade with their light yellow-green framing and integrated timber casement panels.

The building is heated by means of a gas system with supplementary solar collectors on the south-facing roof slope.

With such an unusual spatial concept it might be assumed that the clients for these semi-detached houses were related or at least previously acquainted. In fact one couple initiated the project and sought purchasers for the second unit during the construction period.

Site plan
scale 1:1000

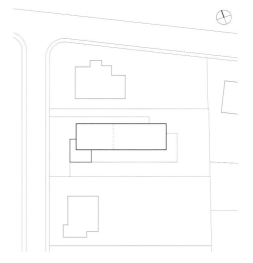

Floor plans · Sections
scale 1:250

A Attic level
B Upper floor
C Ground floor
D Basement

1 Bedroom
2 Gallery
3 Living
4 Kitchen
5 Dining
6 Garage
7 Terrace
8 Store
9 Laundry
10 Wine cellar
11 Services
12 Shelter

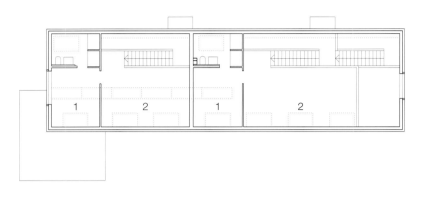

A

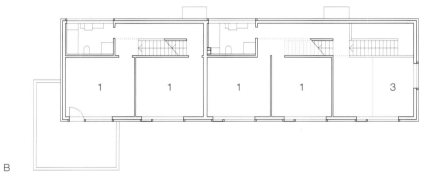

B

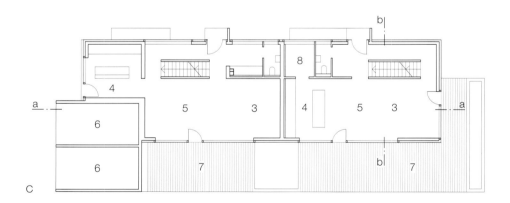

C

Project details:
Usage: semi-detached houses
Floor areas: 1x 182 m²
                          1x 202 m²
Construction type: reinforced concrete
Total floor area: 670 m²
Total site area: 800 m²
Energy requirement for heating:
                          40.8 kWh/m²a
Construction time: 2000–2001

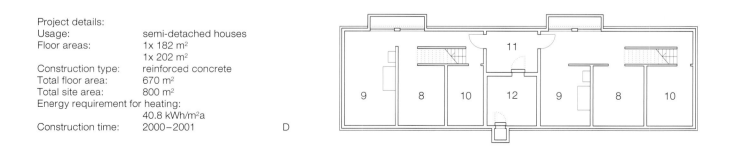

D

114

aa

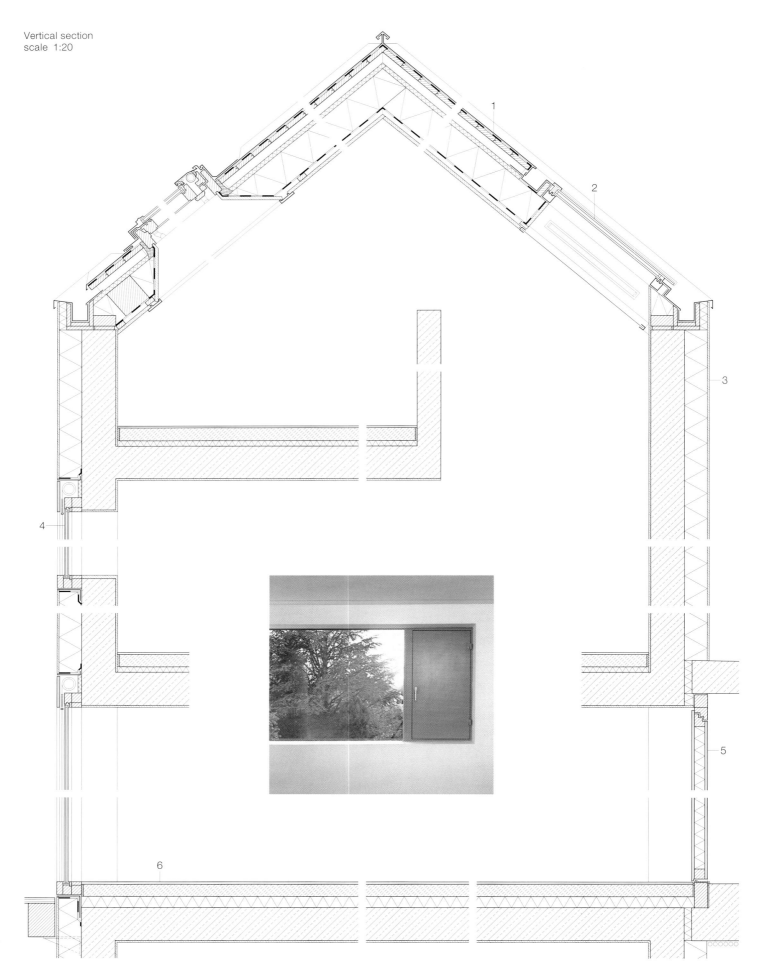

1

2

3

4

5

6

1 roof construction:
  copper sheeting, flat welted seam
  separation layer
  27 mm boarding
  48 × 45 mm counterbattens
  24 mm soft board
  mineral wool thermal insulation between
  80 × 160 mm rafters
  vapour barrier
  24 × 48 mm battens
  18 mm fibrous plasterboard
2 skylight:
  double glazing (8 mm laminated safety glass
  + 12 mm cavity + 4 mm toughened glass)
  fluorescent tubes mounted
  to every second rafter
  0.3 mm polyethylene translucent membrane,

stretched over metal elements
3 external wall construction:
  10 mm brown-pigmented external render
  120 mm mineral wool thermal insulation
  180 mm reinforced concrete
  10 mm internal render
4 double glazing in timber framing
  (4 mm float glass + 12 mm cavity +
  4 mm float glass)
5 timber door, painted yellow-green
6 floor construction:
  14 mm Wenge parquet on edge,
  sanded and oiled
  66 mm cement screed
  60 mm thermal insulation
  180 mm reinforced concrete slab
  10 mm internal render

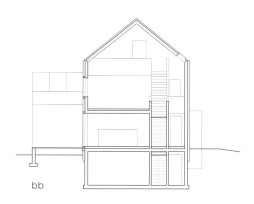

bb

117

City Houses in Nuremberg

Architects: att architects, Nuremberg

Five individual buildings for six clients have been introduced into the landscape of the former Johannisheim sanatorium in Nuremberg. In addition to the restoration of the existing historic clinic buildings and their renovation into residential quarters, the 6.3-hectare site was also the location of sensitive urban renewal: the existing comb-like structure was extended by four single-family houses and one pair of semi-detached dwellings. The new development connects the existing fabric with the adjacent river and park, and utilizes environmentally sound construction techniques. The cuboid residential buildings are located on an undivided 700-square-metre lot which, being free of boundaries, retains a spacious park quality. The views tend to flow naturally between the buildings and the established stock of trees down to the rejuvenated water meadows. At first glance the five constructions present a unified image. While the closed northern facades are dominated by exposed concrete elements, the appearance of the remaining facades is determined by their structural rhythm. The floor layouts of the individual dwellings are reflected in their elevations, by the alternation of closed, larch-clad panels and open glazing.

The approach to the two semi-detached dwellings is via a narrow path to the north. A central entry has been cut out of the concrete building and serves as entrance to both units. The generously proportioned living and dining area flows into the open-plan kitchen space on the ground floor, while the single-flight steel staircase subdivides the multi-purpose zone. The dwellings have different floor layouts on the upper levels, as a result of the staircase being offset by 80 cm on plan. One dwelling has the bathroom and changing area located in a 2.6-metre-wide, north-oriented zone, with two five-metre-deep rooms opening out to the south and south-west. The first floor in the adjacent dwelling includes three rooms of neutral usage, in addition to the bathroom. One of these rooms is located within the northern room-tract and is oriented to the east. A skylight allows additional daylight to enter the houses benefiting the stair and corridor space on the first floor. Services, storage and hobby rooms are all located in the basement level of both dwellings.

Precast concrete elements, fixed to the floor slabs, determine the grid-like appearance of the facades. The infill panels alternate between large-format double glazing and timber-framed elements of untreated larch horizontal boarding, with ventilation cavities behind. The natural characteristics of the selected building elements and precise detailing determine the appearance of the construction. All houses are of low-energy construction, with solar systems, rain-water collection and heating systems completing the ecological concept.

Project details:

Usage:	1 pair semi-detached houses
	4 single family houses
Floor area:	2x 129.5 m²
internal ceiling height:	2.75 m
Construction type:	reinforced concrete
Total floor area:	156 m²
Total internal volume:	1366 m³
Total site area:	700 m²
Construction cost:	1,390 €/m², 360,000 €
Date of completion:	May 2002

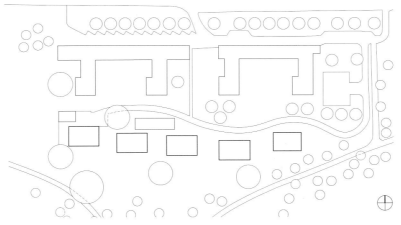

Section · Floor plans
scale 1:400

A Basement
B Ground floor
C First floor

1 Hobby room
2 Services
3 Store
4 Entrance
5 Kitchen
6 Living
7 Bedroom
8 Bathroom
9 Changing area

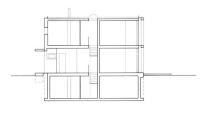

aa

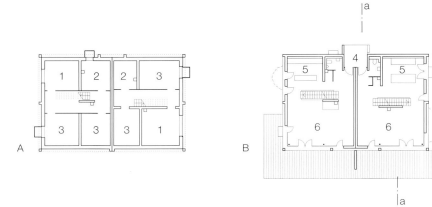

A   B   C

1 roof construction:
   perimeter gravel zone
   100 mm vegetation
   PVC roof membrane, single-layer
   140 mm polyurethane thermal insulation
   bituminous vapour barrier
   200 mm reinforced concrete slab
2 250 × 250 × 250 mm precast concrete element
3 larch window frame with double glazing
   (U-value 1.1 W/m²K)
4 ground/first floor construction:
   10 mm parquet flooring
   70 mm screed with underfloor heating
   separation layer
   35 mm impact-sound insulation
   30 mm thermal insulation (ground floor)
   200 mm reinforced concrete slab
5 terrace construction:
   30 mm Balau grid on
   sub-construction
   gravel bed
6 timber frame element construction:
   24 × 60 mm larch boarding
   24 × 48 counterbattens
   wind-proof membrane
   15 mm oriented-strand-board
   120 mm mineral wool thermal insulation
   between
   60 × 120 mm solid timber construction
   vapour barrier
   48 mm services cavity, insulated
   12.5 mm fibrous plasterboard
7 external wall construction:
   300 mm reinforced concrete
   100 mm mineral wool thermal insulation
   vapour barrier
   thermal insulation between
   60–100 mm services cavity
   2x 12.5 mm fivrous plasterboard

Vertical and
Horizontal section
scale 1:20

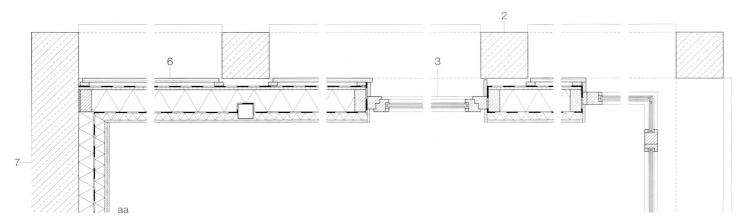

121

Terraced Housing in Küsnacht

Architects: Barbara Weber, Bruno Oertli, Küsnacht

Site plan   scale 1:4000

Some of the most sought-after locations in Switzerland are to be found on the slopes overlooking Lake Zurich. These three terrace houses are situated amongst free-standing single-family dwellings and villas. The density of the development and the particular spatial concept were decided upon by the architects in direct response to the hilly location and in order to take full advantage of the lake views: the split level organization and a variety of outdoor spaces play important roles here. The clear cuboid structure is set back from the street. Each of the three houses has its own entry courtyard with driveway, parking space and garage; the light-weight steel constructions give rhythm to the western facade. The lower storeys, destined to be used as office spaces, elevate the residential storeys above. All levels receive ample daylight, a further advantage of sloping sites. The flat roofs of the houses accommodate generous terraces to the west, while the eastern sides are inaccessible and extensively planted. Both end houses benefit from private, sheltered courtyard gardens.

The interiors of the houses are distinguished by a remarkable spatial experience and uninhibited visual transitions between the individual rooms achieved through meticulous attention to lighting. A central void illuminates and interconnects the different levels, which are set off from each other at half-storey heights. The staircases and ancillary services are placed to one side within the houses.

Although the walls and exposed concrete floors are of massive construction, the overall appearance of the development is determined by the rough-sawn stained cedar cladding, anthracite pigmented fibre-cement sheeting, and the projecting secondary structures of galvanized steel. In the lower levels the architects have once again applied fibre-cement sheeting, here as perforated window shutters. The roof constructions are clad with pre-weathered zinc sheeting. Each house is supplied with its own services plant. The solar collectors on the roofs are sufficient to supply adequate warm water on sunny days.

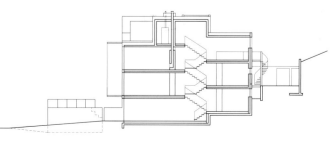

aa

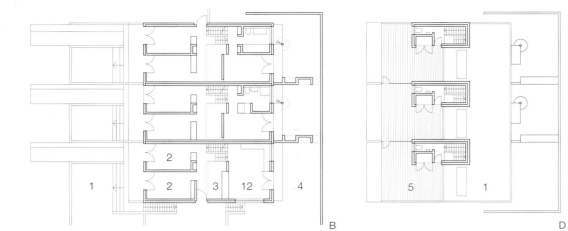

B

D

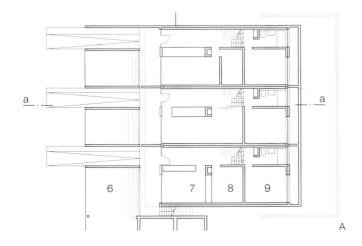

a · ———   a · ———

| 6 | | 7 | 8 | 9 |

A

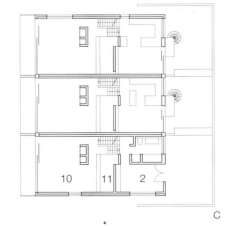

| 10 | 11 | 2 |

C

Section · Floor plans
scale 1:400
A Ground floor
B First floor
C Second floor
D Roof storey

1 Planted roof
2 Bedroom
3 Reading/playing area
4 Garden courtyard
5 Roof terrace
6 Garage
7 Studio
8 Store room
9 Utility room
10 Living room
11 Void
12 Dining area

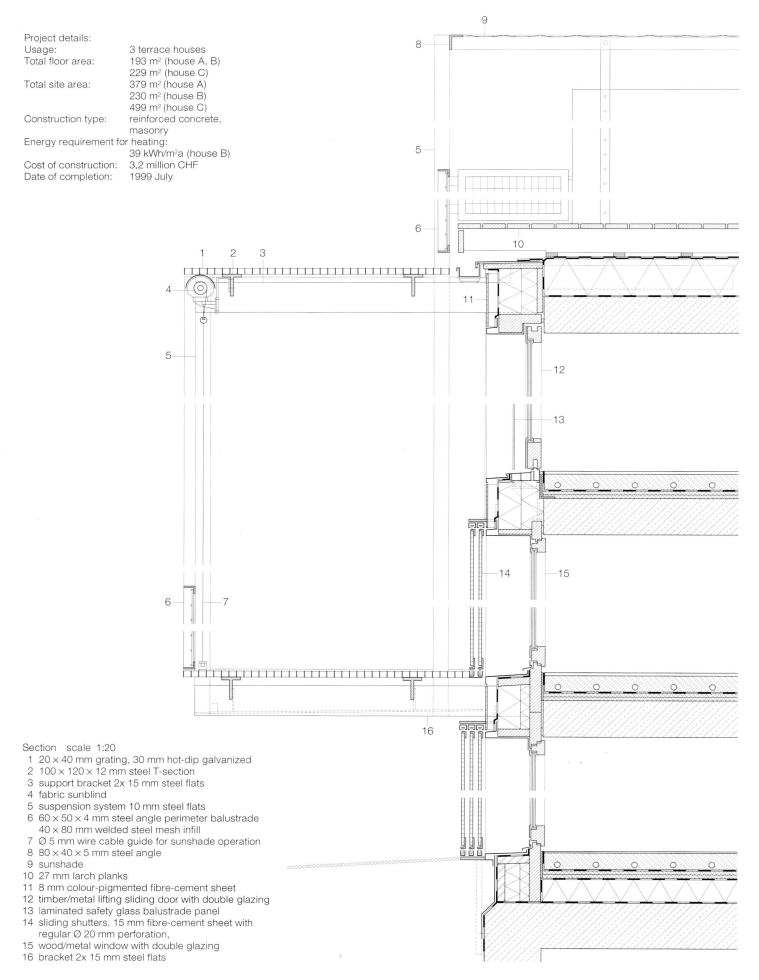

Project details:
Usage: 3 terrace houses
Total floor area: 193 m² (house A, B)
                         229 m² (house C)
Total site area: 379 m² (house A)
                         230 m² (house B)
                         499 m² (house C)
Construction type: reinforced concrete,
                         masonry
Energy requirement for heating:
                         39 kWh/m²a (house B)
Cost of construction: 3,2 million CHF
Date of completion: 1999 July

Section   scale 1:20
  1 20 × 40 mm grating, 30 mm hot-dip galvanized
  2 100 × 120 × 12 mm steel T-section
  3 support bracket 2x 15 mm steel flats
  4 fabric sunblind
  5 suspension system 10 mm steel flats
  6 60 × 50 × 4 mm steel angle perimeter balustrade
     40 × 80 mm welded steel mesh infill
  7 Ø 5 mm wire cable guide for sunshade operation
  8 80 × 40 × 5 mm steel angle
  9 sunshade
10 27 mm larch planks
11 8 mm colour-pigmented fibre-cement sheet
12 timber/metal lifting sliding door with double glazing
13 laminated safety glass balustrade panel
14 sliding shutters, 15 mm fibre-cement sheet with
     regular Ø 20 mm perforation,
15 wood/metal window with double glazing
16 bracket 2x 15 mm steel flats

124

Terraced Housing in Göppingen

Architects: Wick + Partner, Stuttgart

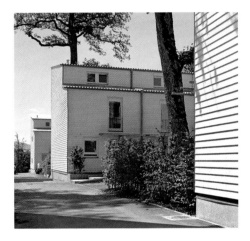

The densification and urban revitalization of this residential quarter – former US military housing built in the 1950s – has been achieved by introducing additional rows of houses. The dwellings are set amid a magnificent stock of mature trees which demanded particular consideration during both the planning and construction periods of the project. The result is a vehicle-free development within a park-like environment, constructed on a limited budget and funded by the state of Baden-Württemberg.

Centrally located on the primary access road, the parking is separated from the residential areas, providing safe pedestrian, play and communication zones immediately adjacent to the dwellings. The public green zones are interconnected by bicycle tracks and footpaths.

The three-storey houses, based on a grid of 4.60 metres, are set out in linear tracts consisting of three, four or five units of 110 m² each. Although the individual dwellings are separated from each other at ground level by hornbeam hedges, the open character of the landscaping prevails.

The architects sought to lay out the houses in groups and simultaneously, to retain their individual legibility. Espaliers for climbing plants are mounted on the fronts of the buildings to encourage visual groupings while, contrastingly, the south facades of the residences are articulated vertically by centrally positioned French windows. Individual entrances are marked by small porches.

Economically applied swaths of colour accentuate the otherwise white, horizontal timber cladding of the buildings. Beneath the continuous cladding, however, a mixed form of construction has been executed. The basement level and floor slabs are constructed of reinforced concrete, while the party walls consist of a double skin of sand-lime bricks. In contrast, the storey-high facade elements and the timber panel roofs are prefabricated and assembled on site.

Project details:
Usage:	36 terrace houses
Floor areas:	18 × 108 m² (middle house)
	18 × 133 m² (end house)
Total residential area:	3,950 m²
Total floor area:	5,240 m²
Total site area:	9,700 m²
Construction type:	timber-panel construction, masonry
Energy requirement for heating:	
	4,752 kWh/a (middle house)
	5,852 kWh/a (end house)
Cost of construction:	4.6 million €
Date of completion:	1999

Site plan
scale 1:2500

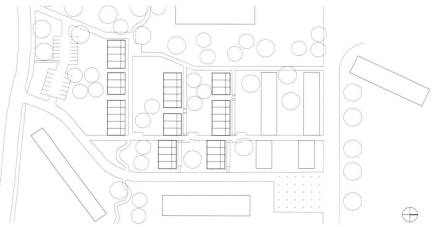

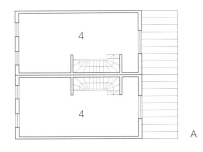

A

B

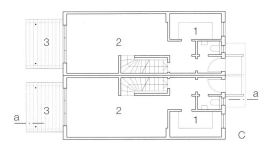

C

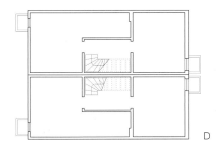

D

Floor plans
Section
scale 1:250

A Attic storey
B Upper floor
C Ground floor
D Basement

1 Kitchen
2 Living/Dining
3 Terrace
4 Bedroom
5 Bathroom

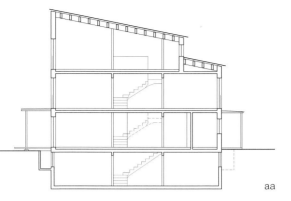

aa

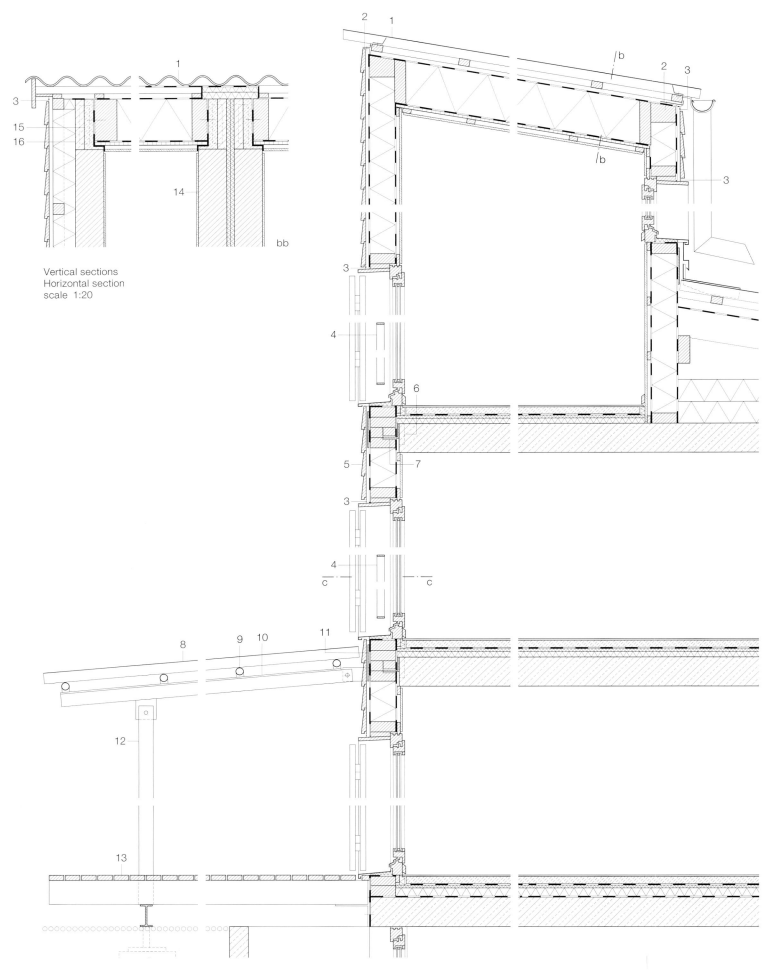

1

3

15

16

14

bb

Vertical sections
Horizontal section
scale 1:20

2 1

b

2 3

b

3

3

4

6

5 7

3

4

c ——————— c

8   9 10   11

12

13

130

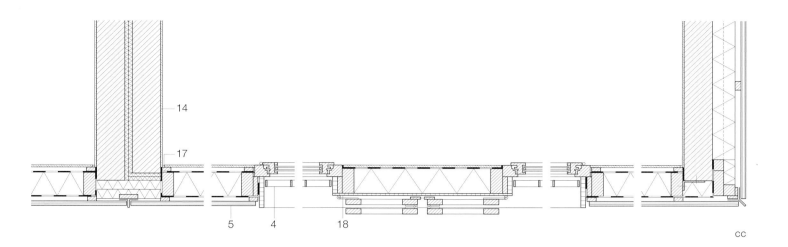

cc

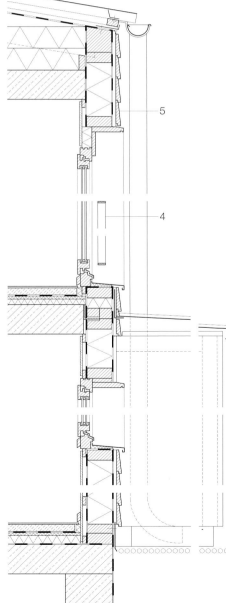

1 roof construction:
corrugated fibre-cement sheets
40 × 60 mm battens
24 × 48 mm counterbattens
sealing layer
240 mm thermal insulation between
60 × 240 mm rafters, vapour barrier
15 mm oriented-strand board bracing
28 × 48 mm battens
12.5 mm gypsum fibreboard
2 ventilation angle
3 insect screen
4 balustrade element: 8 × 35 mm steel flats
5 wall construction:
26 × 146 mm shiplap boarding
24 × 28 mm battens, ventilated cavity
sealing layer
140 mm mineral-fibre thermal insulation
between 140 × 60 mm wood rails

vapour barrier
24 × 48 mm battens
12.5 mm gypsum fibreboard
6 fixing strip set vertically
7 angle connector
8 18 × 76 mm colourless corrugated
acrylic glass
9 Ø 54 × 5 mm tubular steel section
10 80 mm steel T-section
11 80 × 200 × 10 mm metal plate
with lug welded on
12 Ø 76 × 1.5 mm tubular steel column
13 30 × 80 mm softwood slat paving on
80 × 140 mm softwood bearers
14 150 mm sand-lime brick skin
15 concrete grouting after roof assembly
16 precast concrete element
17 smoothed joint
18 12 mm cement-bonded chipboard

Housing Development in Gouda

Architects: KCAP architects & planners, Rotterdam

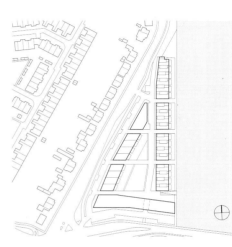

As part of a small housing development in Gouda, in the Netherlands, these terrace houses benefit from direct access to an idyllic watercourse. Subdivided into four blocks – three blocks of four houses and one block of six – the dwellings are stretched the length of the longest side of a triangular site. This elongated, three-storey development is shielded from a nearby, heavily used roadway by a tall residential building. The entire site area is built over at the ground-floor level, whereas the first floor and roof level of the dwellings include various terraces and loggias which have been cut out of the building mass. The resultant variations in height and depth simultaneously animate the facades and allow light to penetrate deep into the interiors. Generously glazed facades to the east open the dwellings onto small gardens, the jetty and waterfront, while the main entrances are recessed into the street facades and open out to a communal, neighbourhood zone.

Adjacent to the entrance on the ground floor are the kitchen and large living area, in addition to the integrated garage. A single-flight stair provides access to the first floor, where the bathroom and two bedrooms are to be found. An extra zone for play or study in the form of a wide corridor, and two loggia-style terraces complete the storey. A generously proportioned central void interconnects the various storeys and illuminates the central zone of the ground floor. An additional room and the roof terrace are located on the uppermost level. All load-bearing walls are of sand-lime masonry and the double-leaf construction of the party walls fulfils all requirements of sound insulation and fire protection. Clinker facebrickwork was selected for the external walls, with only the ground floor facades to the street being clad in red cedar boarding. The windows are mounted flush with the facades.

Project details:

Usage:	18 terrace houses, type a	
	8 terrace houses, type b	
	26 single-storey	Site plan
	apartments	scale 1:4000
	1 commercial unit	
Construction type:	masonry	Floor plans
	reinforced concrete	Sections
Floor area:	200 m² (3-room)	scale 1:400
Total internal volume:	500 m³ per unit	
Internal ceiling height:	2.4 – 2.58 m	
Cost of construction:	15 million €	A Roof level
Date of completion:	2001	B First floor
		C Ground floor

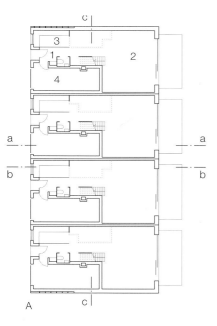
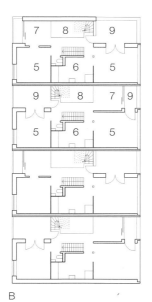
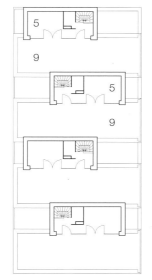

aa   bb   cc

A   B   C

1 Entrance
2 Living
3 Kitchen
4 Garage
5 Bedroom
6 Bathroom
7 Corridor
8 Void
9 Terrace

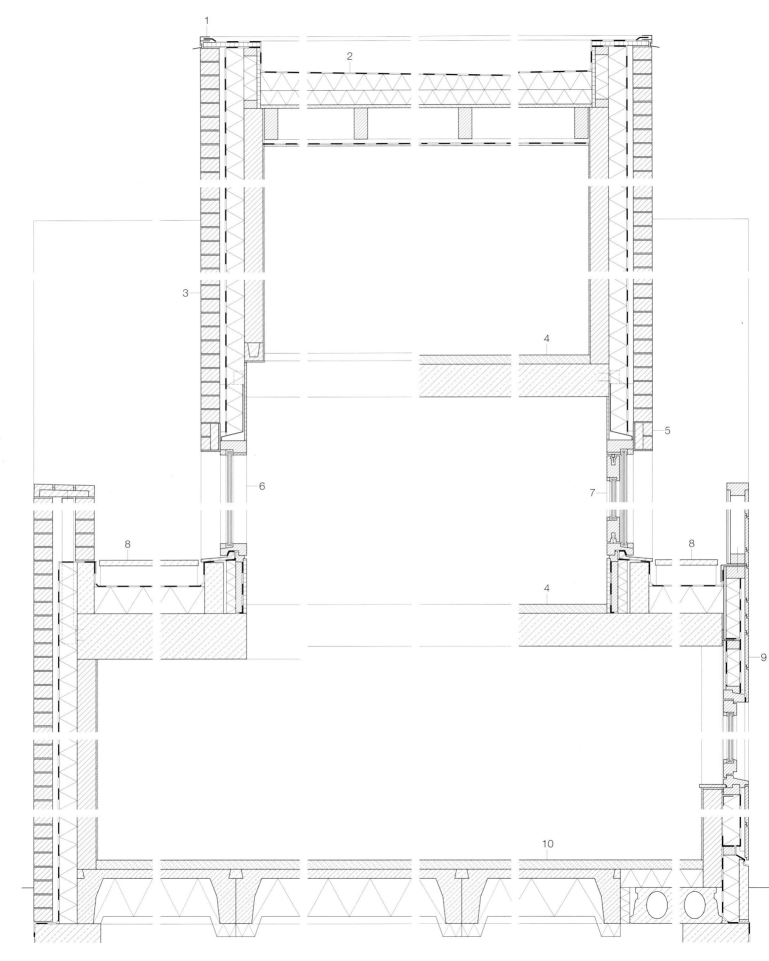

Detail section · East facade section
scale 1:20
1 aluminium parapet flashing
2 roof construction:
  bituminous membrane
  insulation with gradient
  80 mm thermal insulation, 18 mm screed
  71 × 171 mm timber beams
  vapour barrier, 27 × 44 mm battens
  12.5 mm plasterboard
3 wall construction:
  100 mm clinker face-brickwork
  on steel brackets
  35 mm ventilation cavity
  wind proofing membrane
  95 mm thermal insulation
  100 mm sand-lime brickwork,
  5 mm internal render
4 first floor construction:

50 mm screed
180 mm reinforced concrete slab
5 brick window lintel on precast
  concrete element
6 timber window with double glazing
7 sliding door with double glazing
8 terrace construction:
  300 × 300 × 40 mm concrete pavers on
  sub-construction, bituminous membrane
  70–150 mm insulation with gradient
  180 or 250 mm reinforced concrete slab
9 wall construction:
  19 mm cedar boarding, 27 × 44 mm battens
  wind-proofing membrane
  95 mm thermal insulation
  vapour barrier, 12.5 mm plasterboard
10 ground floor construction:
  50 mm screed, 300 mm precast reinforced
  concrete element with perimeter insulation

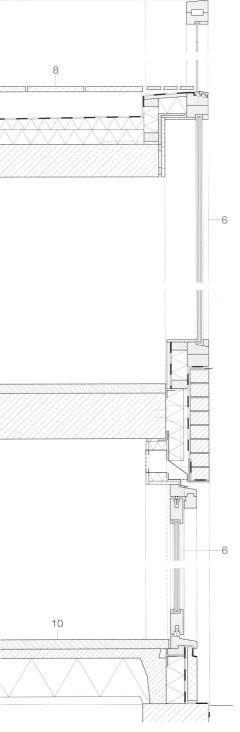

Housing Development in Neu-Ulm

Architect: G.A.S.-Sahner Architects, Stuttgart

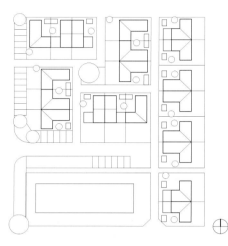

Site plan
scale 1:1500

LBS system house modules
A Minimum volume
B Extension modules
C Maximum volumes

South of Neu-Ulm one comes across extensive areas of land that were formerly occupied by military barracks. The existing structures, whether deserted, forgotten military buildings or new constructions, appear to have been placed randomly within this expanse of fallow land without any thought to urban layout. Situated on the edge of the former military area, adjoining agricultural land, is this modest residential development of twenty houses. They are the result of a building society competition for the design and development of a low-cost, environmentally friendly house construction system. The urban development claims a high density – a floor-space index of 0.8 – yet conveys a sense of human scale reminiscent of village structures with a central open "green" and interconnecting lanes. The development plan was drawn up by the architect and developer in collaboration with local authorities, and received specific exemption in the overlapping of setback areas. The small entrance courtyards to the L-shaped houses and the associated garden sheds provide an important element of privacy for the residents. At first glance it is not evident that all the houses have an identical ground-floor layout and are developed from the same modular construction system. With their various roof forms and the scope they provide for different groupings, the houses create an interesting and polymorphic ensemble.

The fundamental principle behind the development is, of course, the basic construction module of the individual houses which is capable of providing floor layouts ranging from 70 to 130 m². The minimum volume comprises two rooms and a staircase, with a kitchen, bathroom and WC linked to a central services core. This nucleus can be extended by adding further individual rooms. The maximum volume is a seven-room dwelling extending over three floors. The rooms are similar in size and form, so that the houses can accommodate a wide range of user requirements. If required, a self-contained ground-floor apartment can also be divided off at a later date without major constructional intervention. Other variations are possible with the addition of basement spaces and the selection of different roof elements.

The construction modules themselves are predominantly prefabricated and consist of a fixed range of components, for example a pre-selected window schedule. This modular construction system of large-format, dimensionally precise wall and ceiling elements makes simple connections and a chiefly dry form of construction possible, reducing construction time on site. The exterior carcass of a house can be completed on site within two days.

Project details:
Usage: 20 semi-detached houses
Internal ceiling height: 2.5–4.12 m
Floor areas: 123.4–143.3 m²,
total 9,640 m²
Total site area: 3,879 m²
Energy requirement for heating:
60.83–68.00 kWh/m²a
Cost of construction: 817.26–941.04 €/m²,
1.82 million €
Date of completion: 2000

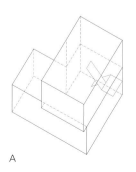

A

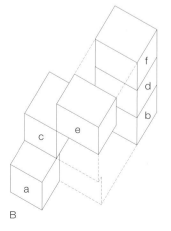

B

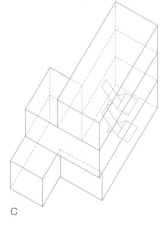

C

Floor plans · Sections
scale 1:250
A Ground floor (house type CX 90)
B First floor (house type CX 90)
C Basement (house type CX 110)
D Ground floor (house type CX 110)
E First floor (house type CX 110)

Isometric view of brick and
concrete elements
scale 1:200

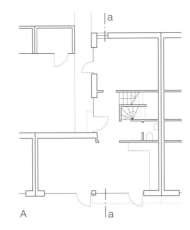

A

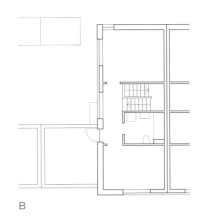

B

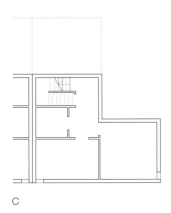

C

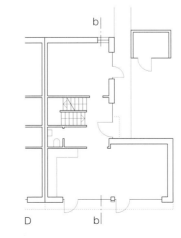

D

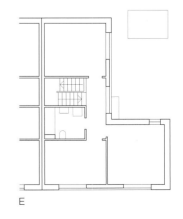

E

138

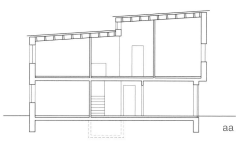

aa

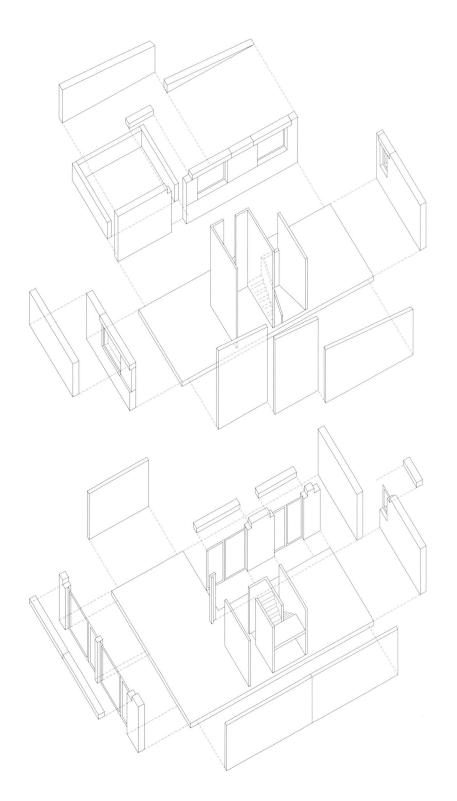

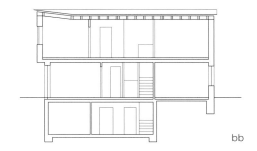

bb

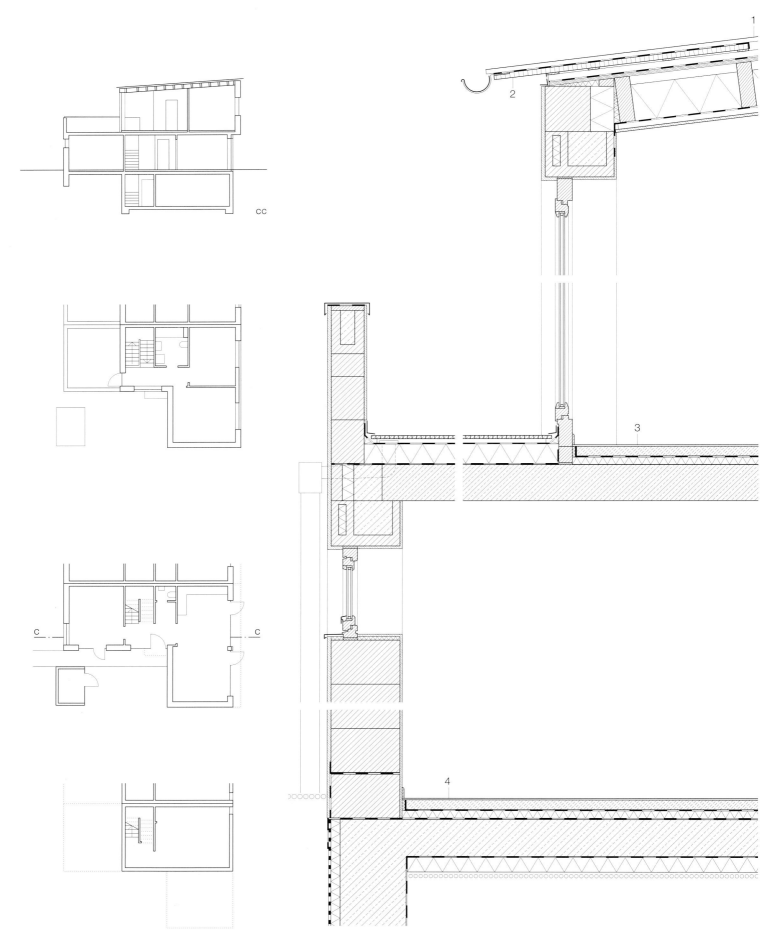

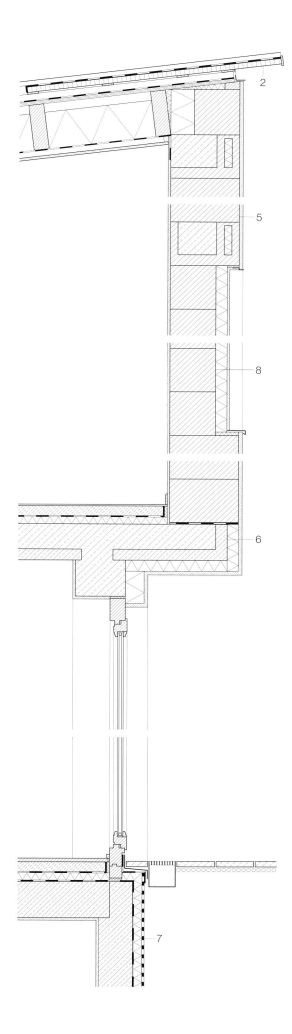

Section · Floor plans
House type BX 90
scale 1:250

Detail section cc   scale 1:20

1 roof construction:
  18 × 76 mm corrugated sheet
  aluminium
  50 × 40 mm battens
  counterbattens
  waterproof membrane
  24 mm sawn softwood boarding
  80 × 220 mm softwood rafters
  200 mm mineral-fibre insulation
  between rafters
  vapour barrier
  48 × 28 mm softwood battens
  12.5 mm plasterboard
2 25 mm three-ply laminated
  softwood sheet
3 first floor construction:
  carpeting or PVC
  50 mm screed on
  polyethylene separating layer
  50 mm thermal/impact-sound
  insulation
  200 mm precast concrete slabs

4 ground floor construction where
  no basement:
  carpeting or PVC
  50 mm screed on
  polyethylene separating layer
  50 mm thermal/impact-sound
  insulation
  waterproof membrane
  200 mm in-situ concrete slab
  polyethylene separating layer
  80 mm perimeter insulation
5 365 mm rubbed-brick wall
  (λ = 0.11 W/mK)
6 precast concrete element as
  permanent formwork with 60 mm
  thermal insulation
7 external basement wall
  construction:
  textured drainage sheet
  50 mm perimeter insulation
  waterproof sealing layer
  180 mm precast concrete
  elements
  10 mm plaster
8 240 mm rubbed-brick wall
  (λ = 0.11 W/mK) with 60 mm
  thermal insulation and plaster
  finish

Semi-Detached Houses in Seville

Architects: Joaquín Caro Gómez,
José Sánchez-Pamplona García, Cordoba

These rows of semi-detached dwellings – set back from the quiet internal access road by a zone of private front yards and parking bays – benefit from views over the lush green expanses of the Royal Golf Club of Seville in southern Spain. The visual image of the development is determined by white rendered facades and timber louvered shutters. A lively inter-action of light and shade is created by the numerous projec-tions within the facades, while diverse minor variations and the reflection of floor layouts relieve the otherwise rigid symmetry. The split level dwellings are arranged around shady internal courtyards which act as central voids, interconnecting the offset half storeys. The double-flight stairwells, set against the common party walls, provide access to all levels.
A small external stair marks the approach to each house; the kitchen, guest toilet and two additional small rooms are located adjacent to the entrance. The generously proportioned living area is positioned opposite the entrance, facing the golf course to the north-east. By elevating the ground floor the basement was provided with daylight. Four bedrooms are accommodated on the first floor, two of which have private bathrooms, the other two sharing a third.
Insulated masonry walls protect the dwellings from the summer heat. Sliding shutters provide sun-shading to the upper levels and upward-folding screens incorporated in the ground-floor facades supply adequate shelter for the terraces.

Project details:
Usage:	52 semi-detached houses
	13 single-family houses
Floor area:	281 m² per house
Green area:	530 m² per house
Construction type:	masonry, reinforced
	concrete
Total floor area:	7,306 m²
Total site area:	13,780 m²
Energy requirement for heating:	
	18.5 kWh/m²a
Energy requirement for cooling:	
	23.6 kWh/m²a
Construction cost:	3.31 million €
Date of completion:	March 2005

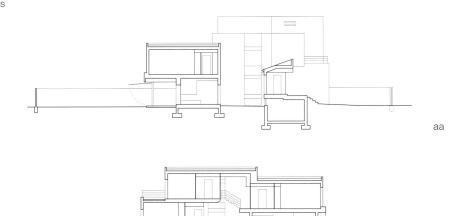

aa

bb

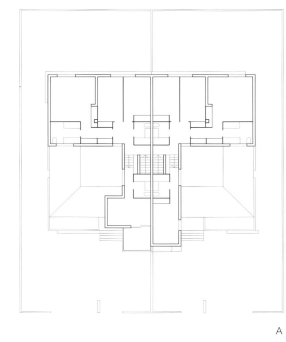

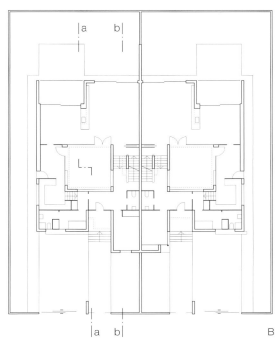

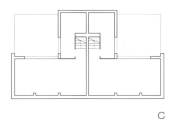

Floor plans · Sections
scale 1:400

A First floor
B Ground floor
C Basement

A

|a b| B

C

1 roof construction:
  50 mm gravel
  70 mm screed
  40 mm polystyrene thermal insulation
  30 mm screed
  double layer bituminous membrane
  30 mm screed
  100 mm screed with gradient
  vapour barrier
  300 mm reinforced concrete slab
  30 mm metal profile sub-construction
  19 mm plasterboard
2 wall construction:
  20 mm external render

  115 mm perforated brickwork
  20 mm render
  ventilation cavity
  46 mm rock wool thermal insulation
  between metal wall frames
  19 mm plasterboard
3 floor construction:
  20 mm parquet
  20 mm mortar bed
  2 mm membrane
  70 mm screed
  300 mm reinforced concrete slab
  suspension system for ceiling
  metal channel section

  19 mm plasterboard
4 sliding shutters:
  19 × 95 mm timber battens on
  40 mm steel profiles
5 10 mm flat steel lintel
6 aluminium window frame with double glazing
7 upward-folding screens (pneumatic opening):
  19 × 95 mm timber battens on
  40 mm steel profiles
8 floor construction terrace:
  20 mm sandstone pavers
  20 mm mortar bed
  150 mm reinforced concrete slab
  polyethylene separation layer, gravel bed

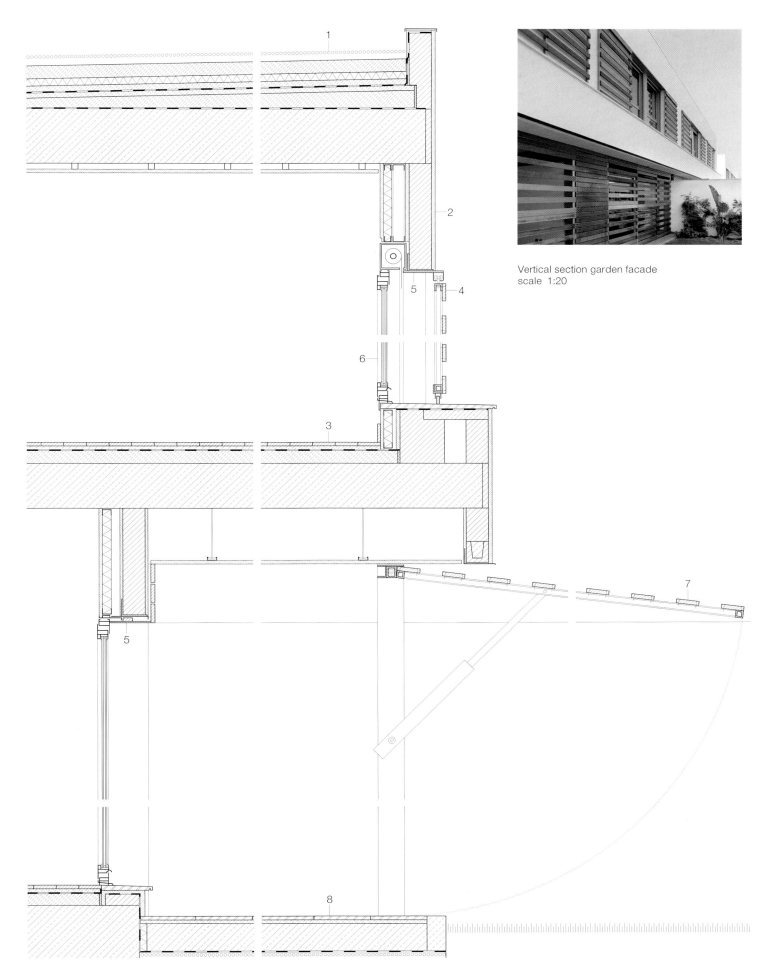

Vertical section garden facade
scale 1:20

Semi-Detached Housing Development in Ostfildern

Architects: Fink + Jocher, Munich

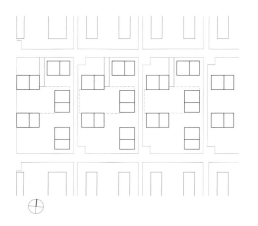

These 17 pairs of semi-detached houses are located in the suburb of Scharnhauser Park in the township of Ostfildern. Lying to the south of Stuttgart, Ostfildern was created by the merging of four previously independent council areas. Utilizing the site of former US army barracks, the building scheme, designed by Fink+Jocher, is subdivided into three blocks of five house-pairs, and one block of two house-pairs which lies on the western site boundary. Underground car parking is provided beneath each of the three larger building sites Although the building structure is based upon a grid, the housing cubes are rotated and offset from one another. In spite of the relatively high urban density of the project, the numerous open views create an impression of great spatial freedom. With white rendered facades, the individual buildings are each subdivided into a wider two-storey dwelling and a narrower three-storey dwelling. Cantilevered precast concrete elements, with incorporated glazed skylights, protect the terraces along either the southern or western sides of the dwellings. Recessed open porches provide access to the houses. Accommodated within the ground floor are the kitchen, guest toilet and large living space. A single-flight, reinforced concrete stair with timber treads connects to the first floor with three bedrooms and a bathroom. Two more bedrooms and another bathroom are included in the third storey of the larger houses. Most of the dwellings have direct access to the underground car parking from their private basements where services, storage and hobby rooms are located.
All buildings are constructed of 36.5-centimetre-thick, thermally insulating, load-bearing external brickwork and comply with low-energy standards. The high-format windows are fully framed with glass-fibre reinforced concrete reveals.

Site plan
scale 1:2500

Section
Floor plan
scale 1:400

1 Hobby room
2 Services
3 Store
4 Kitchen
5 Living
6 Bedroom
7 Bathroom

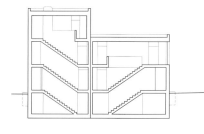

aa

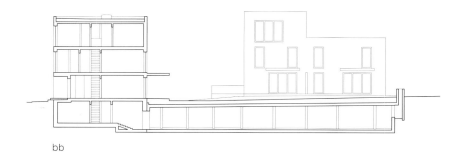

bb

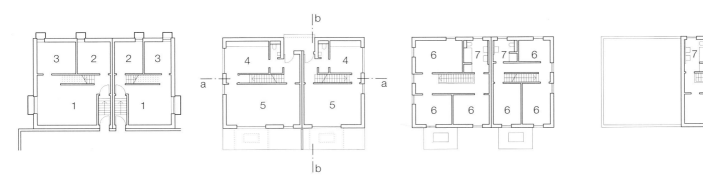

Project details:
Usage: 17 pairs semi-detached
                                houses
                                3 underground car parks
Floor area: 4,650 m²
Internal ceiling height: 2.5 m
Construction type: masonry
Total floor area: 6,063 m²
Total internal volume: 28,600 m³
Total site area: 9,226 m²
Green area: 5,569 m²
Energy requirement for heating:
                                56.52 kWh/m²a
Construction cost: 5.5 million €, 1.180 €/m²
Date of completion: January 2006

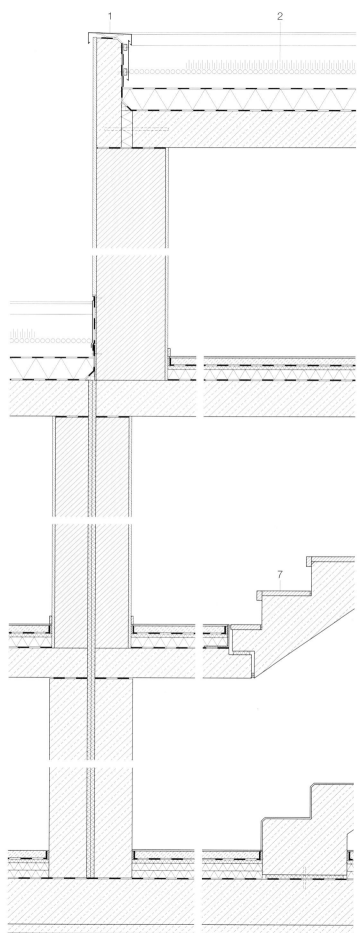

148

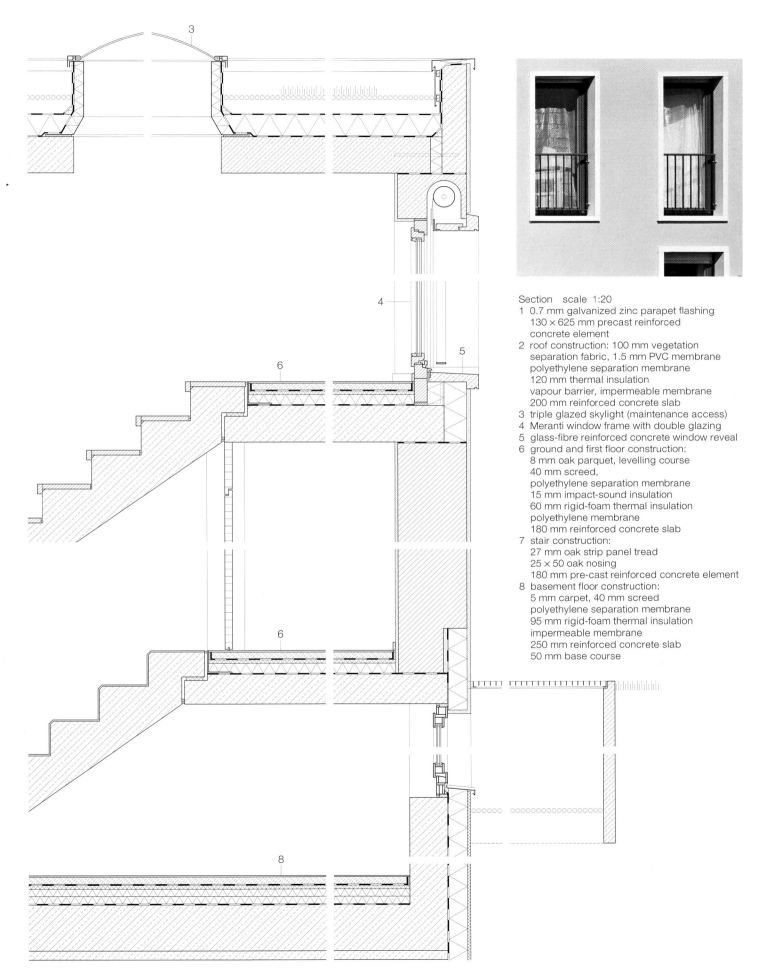

Section   scale 1:20

1 0.7 mm galvanized zinc parapet flashing
   130 × 625 mm precast reinforced
   concrete element
2 roof construction: 100 mm vegetation
   separation fabric, 1.5 mm PVC membrane
   polyethylene separation membrane
   120 mm thermal insulation
   vapour barrier, impermeable membrane
   200 mm reinforced concrete slab
3 triple glazed skylight (maintenance access)
4 Meranti window frame with double glazing
5 glass-fibre reinforced concrete window reveal
6 ground and first floor construction:
   8 mm oak parquet, levelling course
   40 mm screed,
   polyethylene separation membrane
   15 mm impact-sound insulation
   60 mm rigid-foam thermal insulation
   polyethylene membrane
   180 mm reinforced concrete slab
7 stair construction:
   27 mm oak strip panel tread
   25 × 50 oak nosing
   180 mm pre-cast reinforced concrete element
8 basement floor construction:
   5 mm carpet, 40 mm screed
   polyethylene separation membrane
   95 mm rigid-foam thermal insulation
   impermeable membrane
   250 mm reinforced concrete slab
   50 mm base course

149

Multi-Generational House in Karlsbad

Architects: Gruber + Kleine-Kranenburg, Frankfurt

Project details:
Usage: semi-detached houses
Units: 2
Floor area: 1x 74 m²
                        1x 158 m²
Construction type: masonry/reinforced
                        concrete
Internal ceiling height: 3.0 m
Total floor area: 470 m²
Total internal volume: 1,500 m³
Total site area: 561 m²
Energy requirement for heating:
                        70 kWh/m²a
Green area: 326 m²
Construction cost: 400,000 €
Construction time: June 2001–April 2002

This unpretentious house in Karlsbad, Baden-Württemberg is shared by three generations of one family. Because single-family dwellings, semi-detached houses and rural constructions dominate the urban structure of the region, the building authorities stipulated a single-storey construction with simple pitched roof for this site.

The pared-down cuboid structure is surrounded on all sides by a terrace elevated three steps above the garden level. Two discrete entrances with individual stairs are located on the western side of the building and connected to the northern access road. Four additional external stairs, and identical treatment of all entrance doors and French windows, allow for future alterations to the internal layout and the entries as desired. All facades are designed within a rigid symmetry; even the roof has been treated as a fifth facade.

The majority of the house is given over to the family of three, a couple and their daughter, the grandparents being accommodated in the smaller unit which is technically considered a two-storey apartment in the construction plans. Although the internal organization of the dwellings correlates with the uncompromising rigidity of the facades, there still remains a flexibility of structure which allows for future layout alterations. Both parties inhabit the ground floor and basement level, while the roof level is incorporated solely into the larger apartment. Single-flight stairs are located in such a way as to offset the individual levels of the dwellings, enhancing the impression of spaciousness and light. The possibility of interconnecting the two units at a future date was considered; the removal of a wall in either of the two lower levels allows access via a corridor. By distributing the various rooms in the roof level around the central, indirectly lit gallery space, the flexibility of the internal layout has been secured; subdivision and room access can be altered at will.

Large-format, hinged and sliding windows have been incorporated into the roof, which is clad with flat, pale grey, glazed roof tiles. There is no eaves overhang; the roof finishes flush with the rendered external walls, and the grey-painted timber window frames are also mounted flush to the facades.

A homogeneous selection of colours and materials, combined with careful detailing, reinforce the serene air of the house.

Section · Floor plans	1 Sauna	6 Kitchen
scale 1:400	2 Hobby room/store	7 Bathroom
A Basement level	3 Services	8 Bedroom
B Ground floor	4 Entrance	9 Guest room
C Roof level	5 Living	10 Walk-in-robe

aa

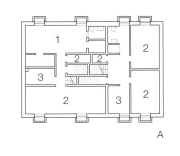

A

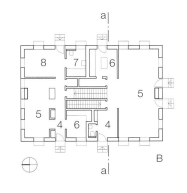

B

C

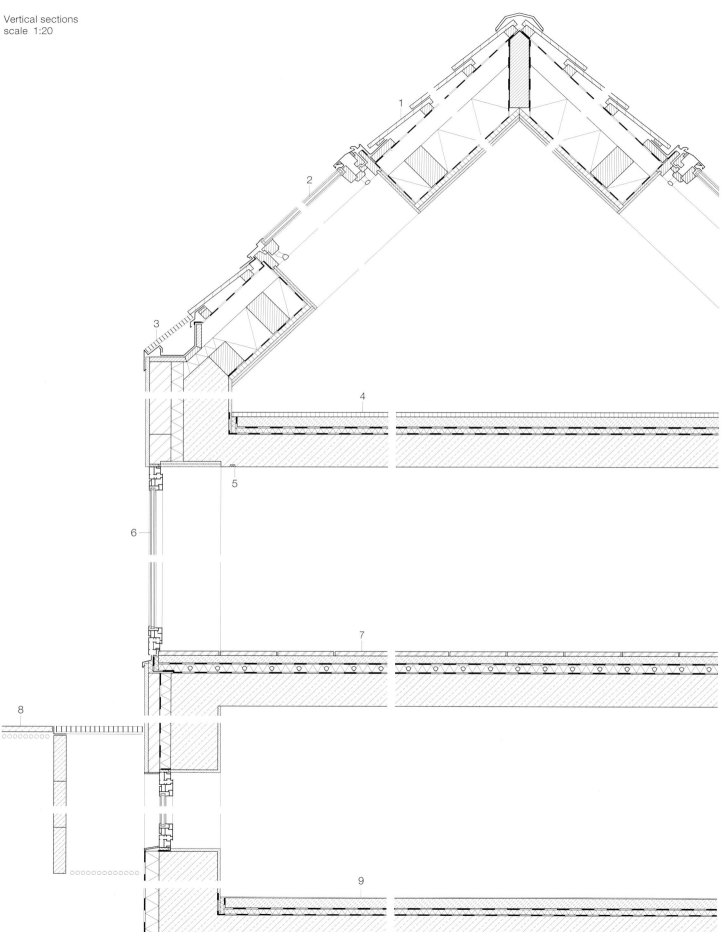

1 roof construction:
  420 × 330 × 22.5 mm roof tiles
  40 × 60 mm battens
  polyethylene membrane
  280 mm mineral wool thermal insulation
  between 100 × 315 mm rafters
  polyethylene vapour barrier
  25 mm particleboard
  2x 12.5 mm plasterboard
2 hinged roof window
  aluminium frame with double glazing
3 25 mm galvanized steel grate
  20 mm mesh, internal gutter
4 floor construction, roof level:
  25 mm smoked oak strip parquet
  55 mm screed, polyethylene membrane
  40 mm impact-sound insulation
  polyethylene membrane
  180 mm reinforced concrete slab

5 12 × 20 mm recessed aluminium curtain rail
6 French window frame with double glazing
7 floor construction, ground floor:
  25 mm natural stonework, 40 mm screed
  35 mm thermal insulation board with
  floor heating element
  20 mm impact-sound insulation
  180 mm reinforced concrete slab
8 floor construction, terrace:
  30 mm cast-stone pavers in gravel bed
9 floor construction, basement level:
  linoleum, 75 mm screed,
  polyethylene membrane
  35 mm impact-sound insulation
  polyethylene membrane
  300 mm r. c. slab, 85 mm perimeter insulation
10 wall construction:
  20 mm external render
  365 mm brickwork, 15 mm internal render

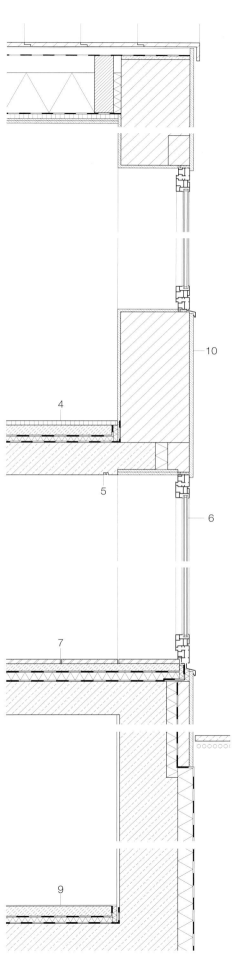

Embankment Houses in Bietigheim-Bissingen

Architects: Kohlmayer Oberst Architects, Stuttgart

Project details:
Usage: semi-detached house
Floor area: 1x type a 240 m²
                          1x type b 240 m²
Construction type: reinforced concrete/
                          expanded concrete
Internal ceiling height: 2.62 m
Total floor area: 597 m²
Total internal volume: 1,791 m³
Total site area: 1,600 m²
Energy requirement for heating:
                          34.973 kWh/m²a
Construction cost: 800,000 €
Date of completion: September 2004

Site plan
scale 1:2000

In a prosperous suburb of Stuttgart a monolithic cube has been burrowed into the sloping embankment of the river Enz, in startling contrast to the more conventional houses surrounding it. Scale and form give no indication of the function or typology of the structure. A pure object with generous fenestration set flush with the facades, it does in fact contain two semi-detached dwellings. The internal structure of the building, as designed by the architects, is based upon a continuous spatial concept which, while very effective, is still flexible enough to meet the requirements of the distinct lifestyles of two families. Both dwellings are rigidly subdivided into generously dimensioned living areas and ancillary service tracts which are located at the shorter end of the houses. The large living spaces stretch through the entire depth of the building and are illuminated by sizeable window elements, while the ancillary rooms and staircases are organized within a separate core zone. Not only the bathrooms and ancillary rooms, but also the cupboards are treated as integral components and clad in medium-density-fibreboard panels.

All bedrooms are located in the roof level and benefit from direct access to both the roof garden and internal courtyard. The foci of the dwellings – the kitchen, living and dining areas – are positioned on the ground floor. The basement level of the three-storey construction is half-buried into the slope, natural illumination being provided by a ceiling-high light-well. The reduced, clear-cut treatment of the interiors tends to direct views outward, through the frameless glazing, to the green of the surrounding orchard and the lush riverbank. The smooth finish of the in-situ exposed concrete ceiling, the sanded screed flooring and the clay-rendered internal walls all harmonize with the warm tones of the built-in medium-density-fibreboard elements. A lime-render applied in numerous coats to the masonry walls is responsible for the lively exterior. The final coat was applied with a sleeking steel and reveals the arm movements of the plasterer, resulting in a random surface structure which animates and vitalizes the external facades.

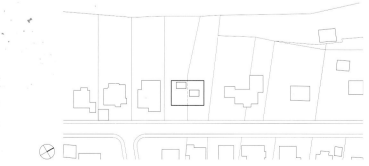

Section · floor plans
scale 1:400

1 Entrance	8 Internal courtyard
2 Kitchen	9 Roof garden
3 Dining	10 Bathroom
4 Living	11 Sauna
5 Store	12 Light-well
6 Toilet	13 Laundry
7 Room	14 Wine cellar

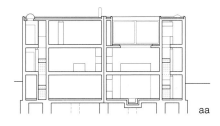

aa

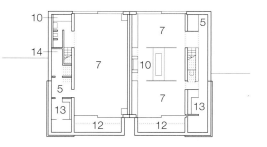

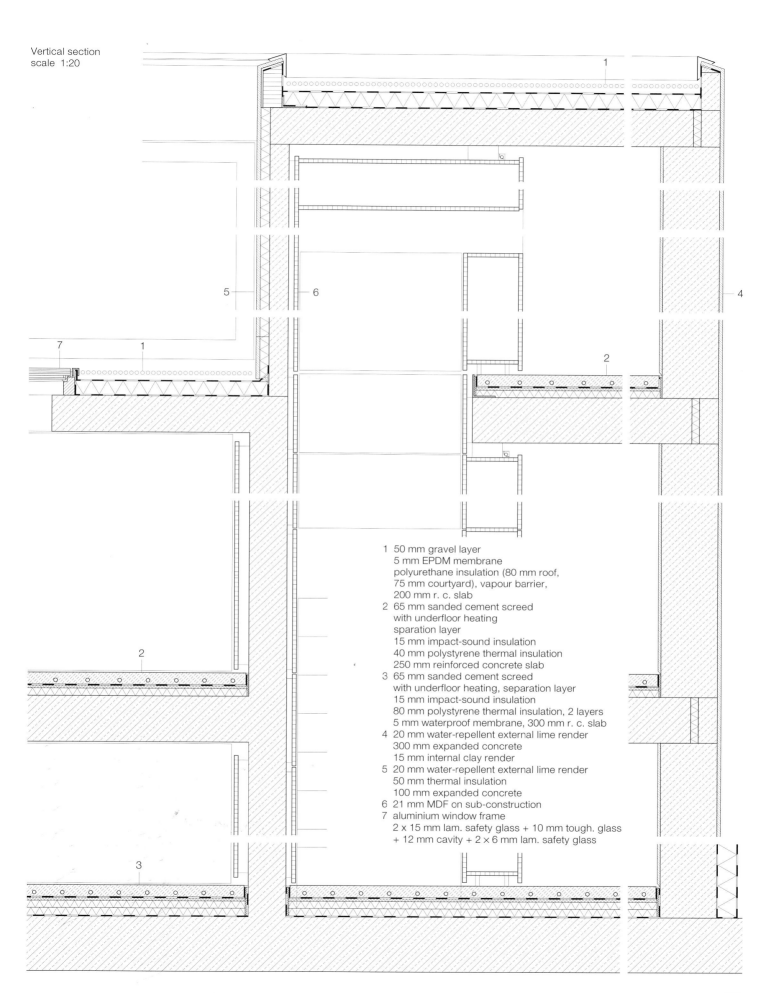

Vertical section
scale 1:20

1 50 mm gravel layer
   5 mm EPDM membrane
   polyurethane insulation (80 mm roof,
   75 mm courtyard), vapour barrier,
   200 mm r. c. slab
2 65 mm sanded cement screed
   with underfloor heating
   sparation layer
   15 mm impact-sound insulation
   40 mm polystyrene thermal insulation
   250 mm reinforced concrete slab
3 65 mm sanded cement screed
   with underfloor heating, separation layer
   15 mm impact-sound insulation
   80 mm polystyrene thermal insulation, 2 layers
   5 mm waterproof membrane, 300 mm r. c. slab
4 20 mm water-repellent external lime render
   300 mm expanded concrete
   15 mm internal clay render
5 20 mm water-repellent external lime render
   50 mm thermal insulation
   100 mm expanded concrete
6 21 mm MDF on sub-construction
7 aluminium window frame
   2 x 15 mm lam. safety glass + 10 mm tough. glass
   + 12 mm cavity + 2 × 6 mm lam. safety glass

Row Housing in Berlin

Architects: Becher + Rottkamp Architects, Berlin

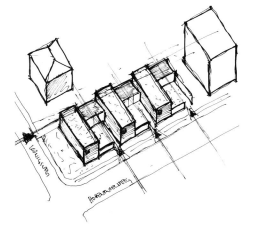

Project details:
Usage: 2 residential/office units
                            250 m² each
                            1 commercial unit 230 m²
Construction type: large format blockwork
Internal ceiling height: 2.75 m
Total floor area: 1,060 m²
Total site area: 1,444 m²
Energy requirement for heating:
                            23.9 kWh/m²a
Cost of construction: 828,293 €,
                            895 €/m²
Date of completion: May 2000

Hard to believe, but economical land can occasionally be found even in the highly sought-after residential areas of Berlin. In Zehlendorf this 1,400 square metre parcel of land was selected by the architects as the location for a moderately priced, space-saving project. The site, which abuts garden allotments and commercial land, was not originally zoned for residential development and required rezoning. The three terraced housing units contain separate wings for residential and commercial usage and include spacious courtyard gardens. This type of courtyard dwelling enables an intense exploitation of the site and high built density while still offering an admirable degree of privacy. In an attempt to achieve an economical and expeditious realisation of the project, the architects decided to do without the customary underground basement level and opted for large-format sand-lime masonry construction combined with filigree precast concrete floor slabs.

The introverted two-storey buildings are connected by single-storey wings along the eastern side. The well executed, larch-clad envelope integrates the various built elements, creating a homogenous yet rhythmical entity and enhancing the comb-like structure and cubic character of the development. Alone the entrances are emphasised by cantilevered roofs in the eastern elevation. The northern facades are closed to the courtyards, with the exception of high-level strip windows, which do not infringe upon the privacy of the courtyards.

In marked contrast to the external image of the houses, the interiors are characterized by extreme openness and transparency. The concrete floor slabs span the width of the rooms, allowing great planning flexibility; the basic module of 6.5 by 10 metres, with a clear internal ceiling height of 2.75 metres, can be subdivided as desired. The ground floor of each house accommodates the kitchen and living/dining areas, while the single-storey side-wings are allocated for commercial usage, office space or workshops. Smooth transitions between interior and exterior are achieved through the application of ceiling-high sliding glass doors with recessed thresholds. An exposed concrete staircase, bathed in light from the glazed roof above, connects the upper level to the entrance zone. This level accommodates the main bedroom, with adjoining roof terrace, and three smaller bedrooms of equal size which are linked by a common hall area. With 250 m² floor area per unit, the houses provide adequate floor space at present and offer scope for the addition of a further storey at a later date.

The interiors are distinguished by clear forms and restrained detailing, as demonstrated by the steel balustrade of the staircase, room-height sliding doors and built-in cupboards of medium-density fibreboard.

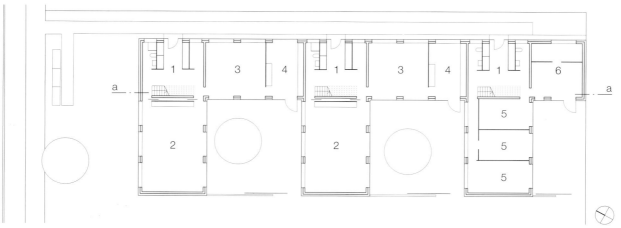

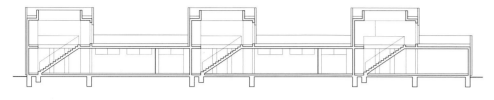

aa

West elevation · Section
Ground floor · Upper floor
scale 1:400

1 Entrance
2 Living-dining area
3 Working area
4 Utilities room
5 Office
6 Reception area
7 Bedroom
8 Play hall
9 Room
10 Seminar room
11 Kitchenette
12 Roof terrace

Section   scale 1:20

1 3 mm sheet aluminium covering
2 roof construction:
   50 mm layer of gravel
   protective matting
   140 mm rigid-foam thermal insulation
   2 mm plastic sealing membrane
   4 mm vapour barrier
   concrete topping with 1 % gradient
   220 mm reinforced concrete slab
3 22 mm planed larch boarding
4 skylight with double glazing:
   6 mm toughened glass + 16 mm cavity
   + 2x 4 mm laminated safety glass
5 3 mm aluminium flashing
6 timber and aluminium window with
   double glazing:
   8 mm toughened glass
   + 12 mm cavity
   + 8 mm toughened glass)
7 wall construction:
   22 mm planed larch boarding
   50 × 100 mm bearers
   20 mm ventilation cavity
   80 mm mineral-fibre thermal insulation
   500 × 175 × 625 mm sand-lime-block wall
   15 mm plaster
8 floor construction:
   22 mm oak industrial parquet
   45 mm anhydrite screed around
   underfloor heating
   36 mm rigid-foam composite sheet
   15 mm impact-sound insulation
   polyethylene membrane
   220 mm reinforced concrete floor slab
9 12 × 55 mm steel flat, painted
10 exposed precast concrete stairs
11 insulating block

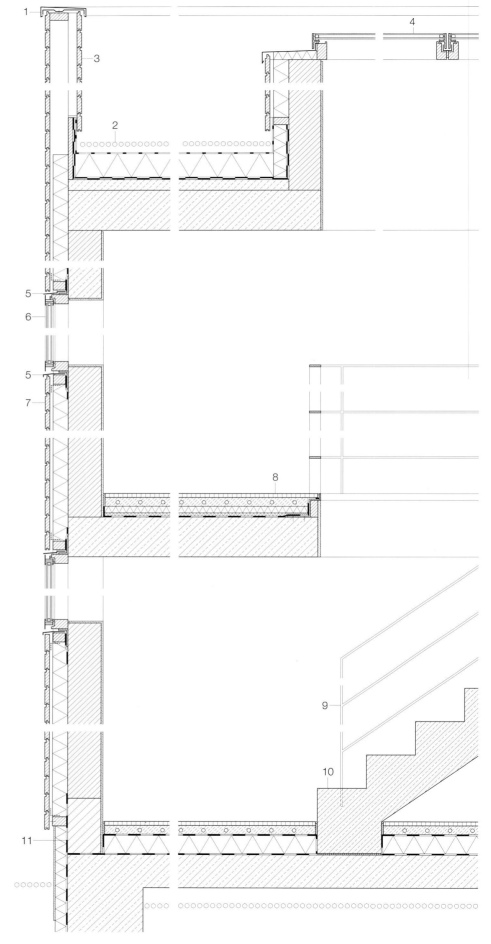

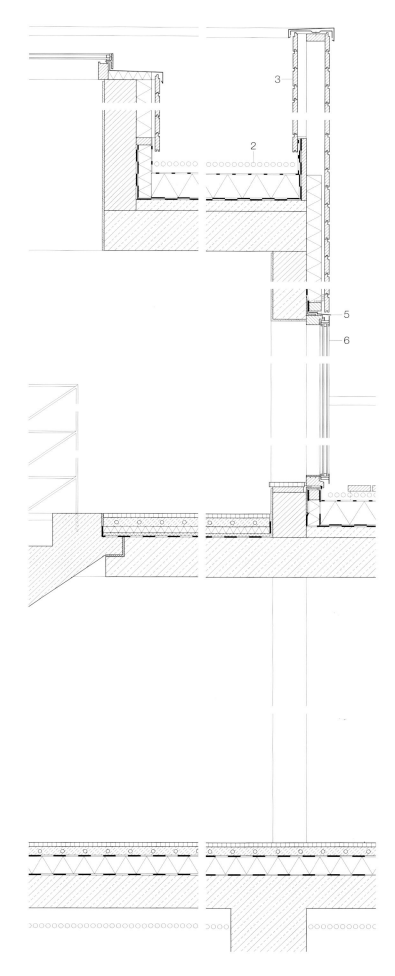